ProHIC
Book of Basics

The ProHIC approach is made up of

— Four combined steps (SAPE: Scanning, Analysis, Plan and Evaluation)

— Five ingredients are key to achieving a successful approach to HIC:
1. Management via the triangle
2. Use of available knowledge
3. Intelligence-led Security (IGV in Dutch)
4. Civic participation
5. Problem-oriented approach: SARA/SAPE

The ProHIC approach is supported by four instruments

— A Manual with a Book of Basics.

— The website www.ProHIC.nl.

— More than 250 Knowledge Pearls.

— Promotional material (poster, handout, teaser, flowchart and infographic).

ProHIC Book of Basics
A problem-oriented approach to High Impact Crime

Bram van Dijk

Paul van Soomeren

Armando Jongejan

Marian Krom

eleven

ProHIC Book of Basics

Published, sold and distributed by Eleven

P.O. Box 85576
2508 CG The Hague
The Netherlands
Tel.: +31 70 33 070 33
Fax: +31 70 33 070 30
e-mail: sales@elevenpub.nl
www.elevenpub.com

Sold and distributed in USA and Canada

Independent Publishers Group
814 N. Franklin Street
Chicago, IL 60610, USA
Order Placement: +1 800 888 4741
Fax: +1 312 337 5985
orders@ipgbook.com
www.ipgbook.com

Eleven is an imprint of Boom uitgevers Den Haag.

ISBN 978-94-6236-258-1
© 2021 Van Dijk, Van Soomeren, Jongejan & Krom | Eleven

Table of Contents

→ EXAMPLE

Police Label Safe and Secure Housing Alkmaar

88

→ EXAMPLE
Tackling Hot Shots
120

→ EXAMPLE
Tackling Residential Burglaries in Gouda
135

SAPE Diagram

Five ingredients key for tackling HIC

Intelligence-led security	Civic participation	Management via the triangle	Use of available knowledge	Problem-oriented approach

Introduction

The ProHIC Book of Basics is not a page turner for a rainy afternoon: it is intended as a reference book that you can refer to when your employer or trainer asks you to draw up an Action Plan to tackle High Impact Crime (HIC).

T his Book of Basics was written by the DSP-groep and the National Police of the Netherlands and is part of a larger European project: Cutting Crime Impact (www.cuttingcrimeimpact.eu). An earlier version (Handreiking ProHIC 2020) was made by expert practitioners from the police, municipalities and safe houses together with researchers/consultants from the DSP-groep. After several demos and consultations, the 1.0 version became a ProHIC Book of Basics. The essence of this ProHIC Book of Basics is set out in the Manual. Both can be found on www.ProHIC.nl.

Knowledge Pearls

When writing this Book of Basics, in addition to the insights from the various partners in the CCI project and Dutch users of the 1.0 version, use was also made of the many studies on the effectiveness of measures against High Impact Crime. Much of the knowledge that has been gained from these studies can be found in what are known as Knowledge Pearls, which are available on the website www.ProHIC.nl. These Knowledge Pearls were created by Jaap de Waard of the Dutch Ministry of Justice and Security. They not only concern High Impact Crime, but also address a wide range of other crime problems along with proven effective measures to tackle those forms of crime.

A Knowledge Pearl usually includes a summary of the knowledge that is available about effective preventive and punitive interventions and measures. The aim is to provide a systematic overview of published meta-evaluations and synthesis studies of proven (in)effective measures and interventions. This enables a policy to be implemented that is based on reliable facts, thorough analyses and compelling concepts and insights from science and actual practice.

The authors would not only like to thank **Jaap de Waard** (our national pearl fisherman), but also all others who provided critical and expert feedback on previous concepts.

Jelle Brands
Leiden University

Hester van Dijk-de Waal
Municipality of Gouda

Paul van Egmond
DSP-groep

Ruud van Es
National Police of the Netherlands

Kaya Franke
DSP-groep

Max Gores
Municipality of Alkmaar

Evert Janssen
DSP-groep (intern)

Kees van der Kraan
National Police of the Netherlands

Bianca Bates-Kreuning
DSP-groep

Marjan Wilbrink
DSP-groep

Masja van Meeteren
Leiden University

Ilse Ras
Leiden University

René van Roode
National Police of the Netherlands

Cor Snijders
InHolland University of Applied Sciences

Jos van der Stap
National Police of the Netherlands

Mirjam Uenk
Avans University of Applied Sciences

Bart Venrooij
Municipality of 's-Hertogenbosch

Monique Verschuur
Municipality of Alkmaar

Peter Versteegh
National Police of the Netherlands

Harm Vlooswijk
National Police of the Netherlands

Jaap de Waard
Ministry of Justice and Security

Arthur van der Welle
Amsterdam

Anton Wildoër
Zorg- en Veiligheidshuis Noord-Holland-Noord (North-Holland-North Care and Safe House)

Dennis Zijlstra
National Police of the Netherlands

Bram van Dijk and **Paul van Soomeren**
DSP-groep

Armando Jongejan and **Marian Krom**
National Police of the Netherlands

Amsterdam
and **Alkmaar**
JULI 2021

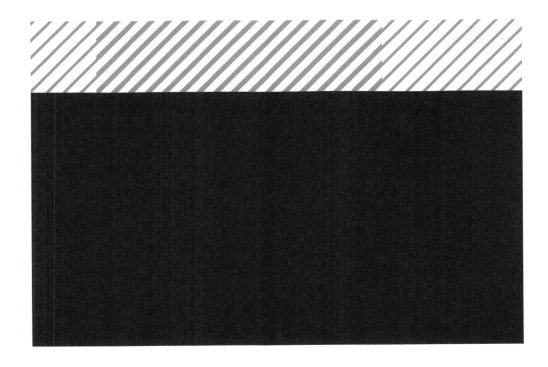

Business shop lifting

1. Why should we tackle High Impact Crime?

High Impact Crime, abbreviated as HIC, encompasses criminal offences that have a major impact on the victim and often also on their immediate environment.

HIC not only causes material damage and/or injury to the victim (objective victimisation), feelings of anxiety and fear of recurrence (subjective victimisation) are frequently also a consequence. HIC has an impact on the perception of safety in society, and consequently on the trust that citizens have in society and the government in general and in the police and the justice system in particular. This means that the approach to tackling HIC must be sustainable.

The following three types of crime are primarily considered to be HIC (as stipulated in the Criminal Code):

RESIDENTIAL BURGLARY

"theft or an attempt to do so, without (threat of) violence against individual(s), in combination with unlawful entry into a home, for example by breaking in or intruding".

STREET ROBBERY

"The forcible removal or extortion of any property by (threat of) violence, committed against private individuals in a public area, or the attempt thereto".

(ARMED) ROBBERY

"the forcible or threatened removal or extortion of any property from an individual in a protected area or on a scheduled or organised high-value transport, or the attempt thereto".

Sometimes more criminal offences are classified as falling under HIC, such as residential armed robbery (home invasion) and other forms of 'excessive violence' (including nightlife violence). A different or broader definition of HIC may be useful or necessary at a local level, but in this Book of Basics, we will focus on tackling the three crimes mentioned: **residential burglaries**, **street robberies** and **(armed) robberies**.

1.1 Scope of HIC

The figures documented by the police for 2019 reflect the magnitude of these three HIC problems in the Netherlands:

CRIMINAL OFFENSE	2019	2020
Residential burglary	39.452	30.650 (-22,31%)
Street robbery	3.783	3.205 (-15,29%)
(Armed) robbery	1.174	915 (-22,06%)
HIC total (2019)	**44.409**	**34.770**

This data comes from the publicly accessible police data portal* (see Chapter 3). The figures reveal that there was a significant decline in these three HIC criminal offences in 2020.

Due to the Covid-19 measures from spring 2020 to 2021, people stayed at home more and were not out and about as much. Opportunities for HIC were subsequently dramatically reduced. See also the "Knowledge Pearls" by Jaap de Waard, number 154* and number 223*. All Knowledge Pearls can be found on www.ProHIC.nl.

* More information about sources, see the digital version at **www.prohic.nl**

Compared to 20 years ago, the total number of criminal offences registered by the police in the Netherlands has declined enormously.

Crimes registered by the police 1948-2020

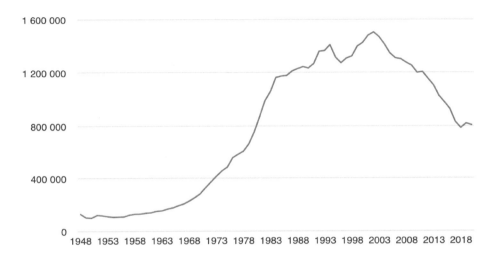

THE DECLINE

We see a similar decline in High Impact Crime. It is also noticeable that residential burglaries form the bulk of the national HIC problem.

High Impact Crimes since 1980

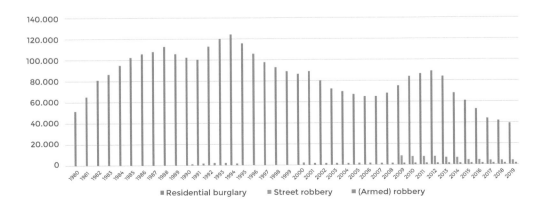

This downward trend is also evident in the figures from Statistics Netherlands' national crime victimisation survey, the Safety Monitor (Veiligheidsmonitor) (**Annex 1**). In 2012, the victim rate for burglaries amongst the Dutch population was 1.8%, and in 2019 this figure had fallen to 1.0% (CBS, 2019).

Although the Netherlands is not doing too badly from a European perspective (they are around mid-tier), there are several countries that perform significantly better when it comes to residential burglaries, among other things. This is apparent from the Fundamental Rights Survey (2021) carried out by the European Union Agency for Fundamental Rights.

We are, however, definitely on the right track here in the Netherlands and many organisations and people - including the HIC task force - have contributed to this. See A Look Back At Ten Years of Successfully Tackling HIC *.
Incidentally, other approaches have also proven effective here, such as including "burglary resistance" in the regulations of the Dutch Building Decree (Van Ours & Vollaard, 2011), the Dutch Police Label

Secure Housing (Politiekeurmerk Veilig Wonen®)and the Business Security Warranty (Keurmerk Veilig Ondernemen, KVO).

However, it remains important to continue monitoring HIC problems and signal any variances. A reduction is often followed by another upsurge, or other changes may occur that are also objectionable (fewer home burglaries, but more home invasions). Getting the HIC approach to work well on a local level therefore requires continuity, whereby we measure the HIC 'temperature' locally and take immediate action if HIC flares up again.

In addition, although the problem is declining on a national scale, we are not seeing this decline throughout the Netherlands. For example, there are still worrying concentrations of HIC (vexample*). Which is all the more reason to tackle the issue in a more targeted manner. This Book of Basics unites national and international knowledge and experience in the area of HIC to help ensure that the decline continues in the coming years and a sustained reduction in HIC is achieved.

If you would like to know more about Dutch criminologist Prof. Jan J. M. van Dijk's statement concerning this significant decline in crime – which has occurred in all Western countries – please refer to the lecture from the "Universiteit van Nederland" (University of the Netherlands)* which was given in 2014 in the IT nightclub (in Dutch unfortunately).

There was another lecture in the same series* about how government is able to make countries demonstrably safer.

For those who wish to test their knowledge on this decline (and the best explanations for it), we refer you to the "**Kenniscrimiquiz**" (Knowledge of Criminals Quiz) about the trends and developments in crime and law enforcement, Knowledge Pearl 109*.

Research on this comes from: Van Dijk et al. (2012), Farrel (2013), Farrell et al. (2011, 2014 and 2018).

* More information about sources, see the digital version at **www.prohic.nl**

1.2 Victimisation and its consequences

Knowledge Pearl 134* shows that the perception of safety that victims of common crime have is often more negative than that of people who have not been victims. The sense of not feeling safe is greater, the ability to judge a situation is affected more negatively, and attitudes to the development of crime in the neighbourhood are less favourable. Plus, the chance of becoming a victim of crime again is estimated to be higher by those who have been victims of crime. Victims also display more avoidance behaviour, both at home and in their neighbourhood. When it comes to burglary and theft prevention, victims of these crimes behave more cautiously and take more security measures in and around their homes.

Repeat victimisation significantly increases the perception of not feeling safe, and the repercussions stemming from the victim's experience with regard to the perception of safety persist for a long time. The perception of safety of victims is most negative among women, young people and people with a non-Western immigration background. Within these groups, victims' perception of safety is more negative than that of those who have not been victims. The same picture also emerges from a lot of international research. For Europe, see FRA 2014, and also see the results of the International Crime Victim Survey (ICVS).

IN SHORT
Not only the scope of HIC, but also the significant consequences for victims are more than sufficient reason to tackle these forms of crime.

* More information about sources, see the digital version at www.prohic.nl

1.3 Summary

High Impact Crime, abbreviated to HIC, includes criminal offences that have a major impact on the victim and often also on their immediate environment. HIC refers particularly to the following trio of crimes:

RESIDENTIAL BURGLARY

STREET ROBBERY

(ARMED) ROBBERY

This Book of Basics unites national and international knowledge and experience in the area of HIC to help ensure that the decline continues in the coming years and a sustained reduction in HIC is achieved.

The perception of safety of victims of common crimes is often more negative than that of people who have not been victims. Not only the extent of HIC, but also the consequences for victims are more than sufficient reason to tackle these forms of crime more effectively.

North: muggings of and by young people

■■■■ Street Robberies in North

In the northern part of a large city in the west of the country,[1] young people were being robbed by other young people. For example, a 17-year-old victim was robbed in the autumn of 2020 en route to Sports Park North. His father said:

> 66 *He was riding his scooter with a friend. Because it was bad weather, they decided to shelter under the viaduct. Soon afterwards, two young guys arrived on their bikes and asked what time it was. My son knew straightaway something was up. The moment he decided to run away, a gun was pointed at his chest.* 99

Another young victim spoke about how he was cycling next to the tennis court one evening when a boy on a bike bumped into him. Moments later, another boy cycles up to him and pulls out a gun.

> 66 *Give me your fucking money, your fucking phone and your fucking headphones.* 99

[1] The example presented here has been deliberately anonymised. Places and names are known to the authors of this Book of Basics. The case study description was based on articles from the media, contacts with the police (national and local), the municipality as well as residents/parents.

He refuses. A fight then breaks out. The gun falls to the ground. After the boy manages to break free from the fight, he gets help from other people in the area. "Yeah, things could've definitely ended up differently", the father admits on reflection.

It is perfectly logical that parents are concerned, also because they can see how their child is anxious in the days after a mugging and this remains the case for a long time afterwards. The story is shared on the app group of people living in the neighbourhood. It soon becomes apparent that more children had also been victims of muggings. They are often mugged on the bike paths or at the places were kids hang out around parking lots, for example. It is autumn, the sun sets early and the bike paths between the residential areas and the sports fields run alongside a canal, through groves and under various bridges and viaducts. The young thieves are usually after money and telephones. Knives are frequently used, and in some cases, threats are even made with firearms.

Police, residents and the municipality

A report is made to the police and, if asked, the police will let residents know that armed robberies on the route to Sports Park North has been reported three times over the past three months. The community police officers are aware of this and try to keep an eye on the area. However, according to the police, the numbers are not high enough to justify additional measures. Residents would like to see more and better street lighting, possibly cameras, and better visibility and monitoring of the quiet cycling lanes. The sport clubs at the Sportpark North also warns their members not to cycle alone. Chair of a sports club:

 All sports clubs here have asked the parents to bring their kids or arrange for several children to cycle to and from the sports club together under supervision. This is not how it ought to be, of course, but otherwise it is just too dangerous. We notice that the muggings are becoming more and more violent and even knives and pistols are being used. **99**

The municipality is also called in to deal with it, partly because a councillor raised questions with the mayor. According to the police, the number of muggings in North is not higher than in previous years. Neither are the figures out of step with the rest of the city. Incidentally, a lot of parents and young people refer to armed robberies while these cases are officially registered in the police systems as street robberies. The mayor responded to the council's enquiries by promising to look into whether there is an increase in the use of firearms in North. Extra surveillance was also promised, and the option of camera surveillance would also be considered.

Parents take action

Because the wildest stories are doing the rounds, parents also decide to take action and also want to get a better idea of the nature and extent of the problem. Some fathers come up with the idea to create a website.

> 66 *The website shows where muggings took place, so that parents and children can choose the safest cycling routes. My own children no longer cycle to hockey practice on their own. They cycle with a group or go by car.* 99

The website provides an overview of a section of North on a map. Every street robbery known to the parents (the website refers to them as aggravated robberies) can be clicked on. Clicking on a robbery leads to a short text about what happened at that particular location (the modus operandi of the mostly young offenders), who the victim(s) was/were (often, but not always, young people on their own or in a small group). The website states:

> 66 *This map shows the reported armed robberies in North. This is how you can choose the safest cycling route together with your children. Have you or your child been the victim of a robbery? Please briefly describe what happened. This can help others.* 99

The information can be directly uploaded to the website. You will then be asked for the date, time, location and whether it was reported to the police. Next comes the question of what exactly happened:

> 66 *Please describe in as much detail as possible what happened. Try to include the following details in the description: - A description of the victim(s), - Description of the perpetrator(s), - Weapon(s) used, - What the perpetrators took, - What did they do?* 99

Furthermore, the name, address and email of the victim are requested. This info is used to check whether all the information provided is complete and whether it concerns a real case.

A total of 17 street robberies are shown on the website. Two are from 2019 and fifteen from 2020. The website lists six street robberies over the last three months of 2020.

Police

The North Local Policing Unit is aware of the website and the problem. Together with the municipality (North district), contact has been made with the initiators of the website. The police are positive about the initiative by the citizens, where raising awareness is a good thing, but causing unrest is not. A number of street robberies occur on the route to or from the hockey club/sports fields.

The community police officers get in contact with the parents and children of the hockey club to discuss their feelings of safety and the street robberies. The routes, parental supervision and extra surveillance were all topics that were discussed. Based on the street robberies that have been committed, it has been determined how, where and when extra measures are needed. Collaboration has been sought with various partners: street coaches, the Public Order and Security department of the municipality and surveillance by and management of the North police department. This increases the number of ears and eyes on the street and can have a preventive effect. However, extra attention is no guarantee that street robberies will no longer take place.

Municipality

The municipality also takes action in North. We quote from an email from the Safety Project Leader, North addressed to the residents actively involved[2]:

• "Lighting in the risk areas and paths would be increased by 30%. This was carried out last month, and the field staff are currently examining in which areas around the sports park the lighting can be scaled up even more. The lighting around the viaduct towards Koeienpad has also been upgraded and this section should now be more clearly lit.

• An order to prune the undergrowth has been issued several times already and I learned just this morning that this has not been done yet. I am not

---

[2] We have anonymised people and places here.

happy about this either, and today I have strongly urged them to sort this out. The sense of urgency was conveyed very clearly in terms of security and the area.

• We are working within the municipality on a campaign that focuses on street robberies. I will call you as soon as this is rolled out in North. As a sports association that has had a lot to do with this type of crime, it seems to us that you would be a good partner to discuss this further with.

• The police have stepped up their efforts in the area around the sports park during the winter months. Other security partners also checked the area frequently last winter. This led to a decline in the number of incidents.

• As to the question of whether any arrests have been made, I cannot, of course, go into too much detail, as this is confidential police information. Yet I can reveal that last winter, arrests were made of suspects in connection with street robberies. As I mentioned earlier, registered street robberies have been structurally low (often 0, sometimes 1) over the past 2 -3 months.

• Installing cameras is not possible at the moment. Because the figures have been so low in recent months (and consequently not proportional), the request for cameras cannot be honoured. In addition, it is very difficult to determine where the cameras should be placed given that no single hotspot can be pinpointed.

One more question that I would like to ask you, as a sports association: During our meetings, we also discussed the possibility of an information evening with the parents. How do you feel about this? Is this something we could perhaps arrange once the street robbery campaign is underway? The dark days are, of course, behind us, but it could be a good lead-up to next autumn/winter for us to organise this together."

When the days became longer again in the spring of 2021, the Project Leader North of the municipality emailed the residents:

 First of all, I'm happy to hear that the sports association is reporting fewer cases of nuisance and (attempted) street robberies. I would also like to compliment the parents who consistently brought their children to the club and picked them up again. The low number of reports you have received in recent months is consistent with the figures from the municipality and the police. The number of registered street robberies and attempted robberies is at an all-time low. Of course, the corona measures and curfew have contributed to this, but it is still very positive news. 🙦

What is noticeable is that not much actually happened ever since then. In 2021, no more street robbery cases have been registered in the system. Following enquiries with the municipal housing manager, it transpires that not a single report was made by anyone. The police had already become less involved with the residents as early as 2020. The police officer who was the contact person, linked the residents directly to the municipality. Follow-up enquiries with residents revealed that they were not aware of this. The contact person for the municipality appears to be no longer as easily accessible - for both ourselves and the residents.

A lesson to be learnt here is that in these types of (usually spontaneously formed) partnerships between residents, police and municipality, continuity poses a problem. What's more, this continuity is very often poorly secured, if at all. If people change their positions and the initial problem is significantly reduced or even eliminated by the measures that have been taken, a successful projectsoon collapses afterwards. This doesn't necessarily have to be an issue, but what if the problem resurfaces later on...

In the last email we exchanged with one of the parents, he stated:

 We have seen no need to do any further work on the matter as we are not aware of reports of any aggravated robberies. This may be because armed robberies have stopped happening, perpetrators have been caught, etc. But we are not entirely sure. 🙦

2. Five ingredients for tackling HIC

The following chapters clarify how High Impact Crime can be tackled. This is done by providing insight into both the knowledge that is available for this purpose and how this is used in practice. A variety of practical examples illustrate the way it is applied in practice. These examples can be found at the end of each chapter of this Book of Basics.

Five ingredients are key to achieving a successful approach to HIC:

1. Management via the triangle.

2. Utilisation of available knowledge.

3. Intelligence-led Security (IGV in Dutch).

4. Civic participation.

5. Problem-oriented approach: SARA/SAPE.

2.1 Management via the triangle

The role of the triangle is essential in tackling[3] HIC.

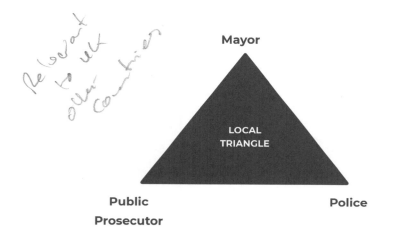

Mayor

LOCAL TRIANGLE

Public Prosecutor

Police

Mayor/Municipality

The police fall under dual authorities: for maintaining public order and providing assistance, the authority lies with the mayor. Whereas for law enforcement, the authority lies with the public prosecutor (see authorities). The mayor usually chairs the triangle and, as such, ensures the coherence and synergy of the triangle. Although the task of maintaining public order and safety consequently falls largely on the mayor, councillors often also have important roles to play (e.g., neighbourhood councillor, youth affairs councillor, housing councillor, etc.). The municipal council, in its supervisory role as the head of the municipality, always keeps an overall eye on

---

[3] Consultation amongst the triangle is based on the two articles of the Police Act of 2012. Article 13: the mayor and the public prosecutor regularly consult with the head of the territorial unit of the regional police force (within whose territory the municipality falls wholly or in part) and, if necessary, with the chief of police, about the tasks carried out by the police. And Article 41: the regional mayor and the chief public prosecutor regularly consult with the police chief of a regional unit. For more information www.ProHIC.nl.

things. Most municipalities employ special investigating officers (BOAs) for surveillance and supervision in public spaces. The special investigating officers in domain 1 (the public space) can play a significant role in tackling HIC. Nationally, there are over 4,000 special investigating officers *(Abraham & Van Soomeren, 2020).*

Since the 1990s, municipalities have been working according to the Integrated Safety Policy (Integraal Veiligheids Beleid, IVB) (**Annex 2**). Over the years, this has become standard policy for many municipalities (Politieacademie, 2013). At the core of this policy is the creation of an Integrated Safety Plan (IVP in Dutch) every four years. This IVP forms the framework for the approach to tackling HIC. The Association of Netherlands Municipalities (VNG) has developed a manual for drawing up an IVP, which was updated for the sixth time in 2021 – "Kernbeleid Veiligheid. Handreiking voor gemeenten" 2021 ("Core Safety Policy 2021", published by the Association of Netherlands Municipalities, 2021). In this method, document models and formats/tools are available for each step. Furthermore, the most important safety themes are worked out in more detail. For each safety theme, the role of the municipality, partners in the approach being taken, and possible measures are outlined. References to websites, models and good examples per theme are also included.

The IVP also provides input for the Integrated Multi-Year Safety Plan Policy (IMV) that is adopted once every four years by the mayors and the chief public prosecutor. This includes themes where an integral stimulus or intensification is necessary and is achievable at the level of the police unit. The aim is to contribute to the safety of the residents of the municipalities that fall under the Local Policing Unit of the police. The idea is to link this cycle to the municipal elections and to draw up the IMV with the new council.

Public Prosecutor

The main tasks of the Public Prosecutor are to direct the police in the investigation of criminal offences and decide whether or not to prosecute suspects and bring them before the courts. The Public Prosecutor is therefore mainly concerned with criminal law and is chiefly offender-oriented and reactive/punitive. However, the Public Prosecutor increasingly endeavours to find a link with prevention, for example by giving community service sentences and other forms of alternative sentences.

Police

The core tasks of the police - under the jurisdiction of the competent authorities (the Mayor and the Public Prosecutor) - entail ensuring the safety of everyone in the Netherlands, preventing and tackling crime, safeguarding public order, identifying criminal offences and providing assistance in an emergency ('to those in need'). In addition, the police have a role in signalling and advising others on matters of security and safety. The police are an intervention-oriented organisation, with a strong emphasis on 'taking action' and often on 'catching criminals'. Area-based organisation and connection with citizens is extremely important in this regard and achieved partly through the deployment of Local Policing Units and community police officers in particular. In the 1990s, Intelligence-led Policing (ILP) (**Annex 3**) was introduced as the guiding principle for the police. This distinguishes between data, information, knowledge and intelligence (intelligent action) (Politieacademie, 2013). Within ILP, scope has been created for police methods such as hot spot analyses and area scans that will be discussed in later parts of this Book of Basics.

Cooperation within the triangle

The triangle also revolves around cooperation. When it comes to the question of how best to achieve the set goals, or how to tackle the identified problems, input from everyone's field of expertise is required. This may involve making agreements on the ways in which the three actors involved are to be mobilised: the municipality, the Public Prosecutor and the police. But also, on the cooperation with other enforcement agencies, such as the special investigating officers (BOAs). The cooperation between the three organisations often takes shape in one of the so-called Care and Safety Houses[4].

Complex Interplay

Therefore, this concerns three organisations that have, in part, different kinds of tasks and each with their own DNA. Moreover, different "types" of people are active in these organisations: thinkers, doers, researchers and inventors.

There are **doers** who put the emphasis on gaining concrete experience, **researchers** who observe in a reflexive way what is happening, **thinkers** who come up with (abstract) approaches and theories, and **planners, inventors and experimenters** who are actively working with innovative solutions. This can involve people, but also the character traits (the DNA) of various organisations *(Kolb, 1984 and Kolb & Fry, 1975).* One key idea of these authors is that there is no right or wrong where an approach is concerned. In their view, it is fine - as is always the case in textbooks - to first plan carefully, then set to work (do something) and then to evaluate afterwards and learn what needs to be done differently or better. But it is also fine to start with the "taking direct action" as long as an evaluation takes place, and something is learned from it that will lead to thinking about a more effective approach.

---

[4] An animated video about the Care and Safety Houses - https://www.zorgenveiligheidshuizen.nl/nieuws/2020/240320_ animatie-zorg-en-veiligheidshuizen. Other partnerships that the police, municipalities, the Public Prosecutor and other government organisations have are with the 10 RIEC (Regionaal Informatie- en Expertise Centrum/Regional Information and Expertise Centre) and the LIEC (Landelijk Informatie- en Expertise Centrum/National Information and Expertise Centre). They support other partners in tackling organised crime: www.riec.nl).

These differences are the strength of an integrated approach. However, precisely because of these differences, an integrated approach can also be quite difficult. These three organisations ultimately work with, and for, institutions/companies and civilians from the civil sector: from housing and neighbourhood associations to welfare work and local entrepreneurs. Although cooperation between the parties is not always easy, it is crucial *(Chito, 2001)*.

2.2 Use available knowledge

In recent decades, a great deal of knowledge and experience has been gained in tackling crime and dealing with threats to safety, in particular where HIC is concerned.

The number of approaches, schemes and projects to tackle HIC in the Netherlands is already significant and continues to grow: from the Amsterdam-based **Top600-approach**, to tackling muggings of takeaway meal deliverers, and from bodycams to becoming "crook-proof". For HIC alone, the website of the Centre for Crime Prevention and Safety (Centrum voor Criminaliteitspreventie en Veiligheid, CVV) lists 300 different preventive measures and projects[*].

New approaches can often be better substantiated on the basis of previous/other experiences that have been subject to a thorough evaluation and research. Based on (international) evaluations, we are fairly well aware what does and does not work. This knowledge has also been detailed in the form of the aforementioned "Knowledge Pearls" that have been circulated by Jaap de Waard (Ministry of Justice and Security) since early 2020 onwards. We hope that the results of the published meta-evaluations (which can be found in the more than 250 Knowledge Pearls on www.ProHIC.nl will continue to stimulate both policy and practice. In this regard Knowledge Pearl 8* is relevant and the many other pearls about "what works (and what does not)".

How easy are the pearls to navigate v20

Based on the results of hundreds of meta-evaluations, there is reason for optimism about what works in the preventive and punitive approaches to crime. An effective crime policy is a specific and concentrated policy: **selection and focus** are the most important features here.

In recent decades, more and more insight has been gained in terms of which direction should be sought in order to successfully tackle crime. The most important lesson is that an effective approach is primarily a targeted approach, as in an approach that focuses on the problem that needs to be addressed.

✱ is this not what they are doing HM

A policy that advocates a general and untargeted approach to crime is doomed to fail from the outset. No impacts can be expected from a more general approach (for example, more police in the neighbourhood). Targeted action may sometimes mean that a specific crime problem is tackled only with limited punitive measures, such as is the case with 'hotspot policing'. Targeted action can also mean that a range of preventive and punitive instruments are implemented, such as those used in a problem-oriented approach. In a problem-oriented approach, multiple parties are usually responsible for the implementation of measures. In the form of cooperation with other relevant safety partners, for example.

2.3 Intelligence-led Security (IGV in Dutch) and cooperation

Municipalities often work with an IVP: Integrated Safety Policy (**Annex 2**) and the police uses the so-called ILP model: Intelligence-led Policing (**Annex 3**). It is especially crucial that the police and the municipality coordinate their policies. We therefore assume a cooperation-based model which is referred to as Intelligence-led Security (**Annex 4**). Also see: Versteegh (2005) Informatie Gestuurde Veiligheidszorg, Stichting SMVP, Dordrecht. And: Welten (2005) Politie in ontwikkeling: visie op de politiefunctie (p. 93).

Integrated work method

An integrated approach is an important principle of Intelligence-led Security. For example, municipalities often have research departments, or contract out research related to security. Municipalities are also involved in measures to tackle HIC, e.g., in areas such as youth services, housing and public spaces. Special investigating officers (BOAs) can be deployed to identify situations that offer opportunities to commit crime. In recent decades, a shift has taken place in which safety in the public space is no longer the exclusive domain of the police. For instance, **more than 24.000 special BOA officers** are being deployed in the Netherlands nowadays *(Abraham and Van Soomeren, 2020)*. Youth employment services and youth care services that are financed by the municipality can also contribute to keeping at-risk young people on the right track (through education, work and leisure activities). When it comes to preventive measures aimed at tackling residential burglaries, housing corporations

play an important role. Not to mention the residents themselves. The local business community is closely involved in the case of armed robberies of companies/institutions; if only because companies are able to use completely different types of resources.

For example, the private security sector currently employs approximately 30,000 people in the Netherlands
(Knowledge Pearl 44*).

Working together sounds logical and simple, but as we have already seen, it turns out that it is a complex interplay which is often not so simple in practice. After all, there are multiple stakeholders who all have different interests, corporate cultures and organisational structures. These differences can form major stumbling blocks. We have summarised the qualitative aspects needed for good cooperation in the diagram below that illustrates the typological ideal.

The cooperative partnership

• Relevant stakeholders work together to achieve their goals.

• There are positive cooperative relationships with the other participating partners.

Cooperation agreements

• There is agreement about the goals, the target group, the intended results (output) and the effects to be achieved (outcome) for the cooperation.

• Clear agreements have been drawn up about tasks, budgets (money and time), responsibilities, authorities and the consultation structure within the cooperation.

Cooperative culture

• Cooperation partners have a sense of urgency.

• Cooperation partners make long-term investments in the cooperative relationship.

• Cooperation partners trust each other.

Management and continuity

• The management and coordination of the cooperation is arranged and endorsed by the triangle.

• The management and coordination are especially aimed at facilitating and strengthening the cooperation.

Information Exchange

• Information exchange between the cooperative partners is arranged in a practical way and does not conflict with privacy legislation.

• When setting up the work processes, explicit attention is paid to limiting the administrative burden and consultation times between professionals.

2.4 Civic participation

Civic participation is becoming increasingly important in many areas. In fact, various manuals (**Annex 5**) have already been published on this subject. In this section, we focus on the role that citizens can play in the fight against crime.

- Two-thirds of citizens feel jointly responsible for safety levels and wish to contribute ideas about which problems should be tackled as a matter of priority (CBS safety monitors, 2013, 2014, 2015).

- Half of citizens would like to be more closely involved in coming up with solutions.

- More than a third of citizens want to make an active contribution to safety levels.

These findings make it clear that involving citizens will increase the likelihood of a successful approach to HIC, even when the real possibility that some of the respondents may have given a socially desirable answer has also been taken into account. After all, saying that you want to actively do something to help is not the same as actually doing it.

It is noticeable that in many of the outlined forms of civic participation[5] where safety and security are concerned, initiatives and the decision-making process for an approach lie with the municipality or/and police.

And as such, not with the citizens. This is strange, because civic participation has since become common practice in social and physical urban management. In urban management, there is even a possibility that citizens might take over work from the government after they have challenged the government to do something. Nowadays, Dutch citizens do have a so-called 'right to challenge' (www.righttochallenge.nl).

---

[5] An overview of possibilities for the police to use civic participation can be found in in Beunders et al 2011 and Jeurissen and Vriesde 2012.

Civic participation in tackling crime

- *When it comes to identifying safety problems,* citizens in the Netherlands have a limited amount of influence. Although the Dutch Safety Monitor (Veiligheidsmonitor, a nationwide victim survey) does ask questions about problems concerning safety, this is done with a random sample that often does not allow for any statements to be made at a neighbourhood level. Several (large) municipalities have their own Safety Monitor, which provides annual insight into the problems concerning safety that citizens in their neighbourhood consider important. In the vast majority of (smaller) municipalities, citizens are required to take their own initiative in reporting problems concerning safety to the police or their municipality.

- *Involving citizens in the prioritisation* **of problems concerning safety is a form of civic participation that occurs very rarely in the Netherlands.** In those areas where it does happen –for example with *Rotterdam/Buurt bestuurt* **(Annex 6)** – the municipality is usually the initiator. In these cases, there is close cooperation with the police and other organisations that play a role in increasing safety levels and the quality of life in the neighbourhood.

- *On the other hand, when it comes to the analysis of problems,* citizens are quite often involved. For example, community or district officers of the municipality may hold bilateral meetings with school principals, shopkeepers, actively involved neighbourhood mothers and fathers, young people, youth workers, the homeless, etc. During these meetings, they ask about the underlying causes of the problems and what, in the opinion of the public, should be done to tackle them. One specific variant that focuses mainly on unsafe places and situations in the neighbourhood is the joint neighbourhood survey (a so-called "buurtschouw") carried out by the police or municipality together with local residents. The concept of the joint survey will be addressed in further detail later on **(Annex 16)**.

• *In the implementation of measures,* **citizens play an important role in three different ways.**

In the first place, when it comes to taking preventive measures to reduce the risk of (repeat) victimisation *(Lopez, 2007, Kunst et al., 2008 and Van Reemst et al., 2013)*. The police and municipality then fulfil an advisory or a motivational role. This can be done without any extra effort by providing victims and their neighbours with information about prevention and burglary-proof measures after an (attempted) residential burglary. The police can do that (a detective or a forensic assistant), but the municipality could also do it or have it done. **Slachtofferhulp Nederland (SHN)*** (Victim Support Netherlands) is a good example of this (**Annex 7**).

Sometimes the municipality offers subsidies that encourage citizens to take preventive measures. This is also the case for companies in some municipalities. For example, a subsidy to install 'high-quality' - i.e., "transparent" - roller shutters or to encourage living above shops (which is good for social control). See **"wonen boven winkels"*** (living above shops).

This usually fits within the broader framework of the Business Security Warranty (**Keurmerk Veilig Ondernemen, KVO)***.

In the second place, citizens can also help a lot in tracking down perpetrators. The research "Meer heterdaadkracht; Aanhoudend in de buurt" *(Van Baardewijk e.a., 2007)* clearly demonstrates the importance of information that comes from citizens. About 80 to 90% of all suspects are arrested in the act. On average, about 70% of arrests made where the perpetrators were caught red-handed are initiated by citizens. Increasing levels of alertness and a willingness to report crime is therefore important when it comes to tackling HIC. Because citizens are sometimes afraid of becoming known as the person who reported a crime, the Meld Misdaad Anoniem initiative ("Report Crime Anonymously") was set up (**Annex 8**).

Neighbourhood Watch was introduced in the Netherlands in 1987, following the examples of the UK and US. It is one of the approaches that has been adopted to involve citizens. The aim of Neighbourhood Watch is to prevent crimes, but it can also contribute to tracking down perpetrators (**Annex 8**). Since the 1990s, various forms of digital support for Neighbourhood Watch have emerged. One early form was Burgernet, which was followed by many other improvements. In the article

* More information about sources, see the digital version at **www.prohic.nl**

"Digitale coproductie van preventie en opsporing met burgers" ("Digital coproduction for prevention and detection with the help of citizens"), Van den Oord and Kokkeler (2020) present four examples in which a digital coproduction between the municipality, police and citizens has been established. The "Borne Waakt" example exemplifies this. Attention for continuity, and therefore proper monitoring, are key focal points here. The "Noord" example clearly demonstrates this as well.

A third form focuses on increasing social cohesion in neighbourhoods. These types of measures are initiated by the municipality. The role of the police is usually limited to cooperation with the neighbourhood police officer. In the long term, this approach may result in a positive effect on levels of safety in the neighbourhood.

2.5 Problem-oriented approach: SARA Becomes SAPE

The **SARA** model developed in England is frequently used when developing a problem-oriented approach to tackling the problems of crime *(Eck & Spelman, 1987)*.

SARA is by far the most widely used model in the world for a problem-orientated approach aimed at dealing with threats to safety. By dividing the entire project into separate phases - in which the steering process can be separated from a strategic one via a tactical one to an operational one - **SARA** ensures that the steps required are taken in the right order. This provides a useful safety net for the

natural tendency to take immediate action when the problem has only been cursorily defined and analysed, and an evaluation of what the effects of this are on the problem has not yet been carried out.

For more information, see:
Crime Analysis for Problem Solvers in 60 Small Steps (step 7, p. 26)*. This book *(Clarke & Eck, 2010)* **has been translated into more than twenty languages*** **from Chinese and Portuguese to Estonian and Dutch** *(Eysink Smeets et al., 2010)*.

Or read *Home Office (2020)* **Safer Streets Fund***.

SARA is not the only model that aims to reduce crime, but it is the most popular among crime analysts. Other models include

- PROblem, Cause, Tactic or Treatment, Output, and Result (**PROCTOR**);
- Clients, Acquire information, Partners, Response, Assessment (**CAPRA**);
- Intelligence, Intervention, Implementation, Involvement, Impact (**5Is**);
- Scan, Prioritise, Analysis, Task, Intervene, Assess, Learn (**SPATIAL**).

In the Netherlands, this type of structured, learning-oriented approach was referred to in 1981 as "**de Stappenmethode**" (the Step-by-Step Method, Oriënteringsnota VM 1981). The road that crime prevention in the Netherlands subsequently followed was rather bumpy (Van Dijk et al., 2017). Globally, the international **ISO** standard on **Risk Management** (ISOI 31000) is the guideline. This is based on the Plan-Do-Check-Act circle (**PDCA**).

Diagram: Based on the ProHIC version of the English SARA model (Annex 9).

SCAN

ANALYSE

- Determine whether there are (major) problems with HIC in your municipality and what the consequences are. Use as input:
  - police data (portal, scan, early warning);
  - a consideration of the levels of seriousness;
  - broader consideration of the overall picture of local crime in the municipality (through discussions with key people or periodic surveys among the population and organisations)
- Indicate roughly what needs to be achieved for this problem by citizens/institutions/companies, the municipality, the police and the Public Prosecutor.
- Choose one or more problems that have been mentioned (prioritisation) together and analyze them in the next step.

- What exactly do we know about the problem/ problems to be tackled (place/time/ perpetrators/victims, nature/size/development) and who are involved? Who is already doing something about it and what are they doing?
- How/why does the problem arise (cause/effect); what causes what?

EVALUATE

- Make an action plan together with the problem description, definition and approach (goals/ measures/planning/stakeholders/bn/sharing) and the evaluation plan.

- Formulate together with all those involved what you want to achieve with regard to the problem, which measures are possible to solve/reduce the problem and choose the best feasible set of measures.
- Why and how could (each of the) measures work? Always give a brief description and substantiation of the presumed effect. Also check out what others (domestic/abroad) have already done/tried.

PLAN and EXECUTE ACTION

The SARA approach (1): takes a broad look at signals: what is going on in the area of crime (including HIC) and unsafe situations (scanning). Following prioritisation process, an in-depth analysis (2): is made to better understand the causes and backgrounds (analysis). After that, solutions and measures can be sought together with other stakeholders (3): an action plan is drawn up that is then implemented (response). Lastly (4), what has been done and whether, and to what extent, the measures taken have been successful (evaluation) are examined.

In this Book of Basics, we follow the same model, but we use Dutch terms for the four sections, which leads us to SAPE:

- **S**canning
- **A**nalysis
- **P**lan of action and implementation
- **E**valuation

In the following 4 chapters, these four main components of problem-oriented way of working are dealt with step by step.

2.6 Summary

Management should be handled by the triangle, which comprises the mayor, the Public Prosecutor and the police. The triangle works together with organisations, companies and citizens depending on the type of problem. So, these are organisations whose tasks are partially different, but it is these differences that form the strength of the integrated work method.

By dividing the entire project into separate phases, you ensure that the steps that need to be taken are carried out in the correct order. Think in terms of SAPE:

• Scanning

• Analysis

• Action plan and implementation

• Evaluation

Intelligence-led Security (ILS) is based on an integrated way of working. This involves stakeholders who have, in part, a variety of interests and concerns. As these differences could potentially form a stumbling block, it is therefore useful to look at the qualitative aspects that are needed for good cooperation.

By involving citizens, companies and organisations, the chances of being able to successfully tackle HIC are heightened. This can be done in different ways or at different times through:

• Scanning

• Decision-making

• Analysis of the problem

• Implementation

Borne Waakt Neighbourhood Watch

Borne is a small municipality of about 25,000 residents in the Eastern part of the Netherlands near the German border. As early as 2015, a group of citizens in Borne started systematically organising neighbourhood watch activities. The reason for this was that many citizens did not feel safe and those involved in the initiative had been victims of break-ins. The perception of not feeling safe is mainly due to the fact that, as a close-knit and quiet community, Borne is wedged between two highways - the A1 and the A35. Both roads offer quick escape routes for burglars and other criminals to the Randstad and Germany. In setting up the initiative and the app communities, the initiators took a good look at experiences elsewhere.

Together

From the outset, cooperation was sought and successfully found with the police and the local press. The support of the police and good press resulted in a lot of positive reactions from local residents. A website was set up* where residents could register, after which they were admitted to the

* More information about sources, see the digital version at http://bornewaakt.nl

online community following a quick verification. BorneWaakt! now consists of seventeen app groups of approx. 150 people, each of whom are active in ten neighbourhoods. The administrators of those groups are the linking pins in a joint app group and head the frequently-held municipality-wide meetings. The administrators see to it that communication remains as goal-oriented as possible and does not become bogged down by everyday petty matters. They do realise that the use of WhatsApp tends to facilitate this. Alternatives are also being sought that meet the same principles where low costs and simplicity of use are concerned. The expectation is that the group will continue to work with regular social media outlets for some time yet. All the more so because there are no professionals participating in these groups. The groups are by and for citizens, albeit some police officers are involved as private individuals.

Coordination

Communication and coordination with the police and the municipality takes place during regular informal meetings between a number of group managers, community officers and experts from the municipality's Public Order and Security department. In these consultations, a new policy practice is gradually developing that is driven by the accessibility of digital data. The use of peer-to-peer notifications via app-groups is wholly focused on prevention. As soon as the group managers believe that there is a valid reason to report a criminal case, the citizen in question is encouraged to report it directly to the police. People realise that it is sometimes difficult to draw the line between prevention and detection. A few years ago, dubious door-to-door salespeople and suppliers of all kinds of services regularly turned up in various districts of Borne in vans with foreign number plates. Reports of these incidents spread through the app like wildfire. However, it was not only concerned textual descriptions, but photos of vans and license plates were shared as well. Another example was the search for a missing child, who app members were able to find faster than the police could. At that point, the number of messages being shared increased exponentially (with no photos being shared as far as the administrators knew).

Expansion?

Expansion of the app groups with new data collection technology (such as cameras) is not yet on the agenda. At the same time, it is unknown to the administrators how many cameras, digital doorbells and dashcams are already being used by residents. The data flow in the app groups is improved by the fact that district police officers in the coordination meetings, or via the joint app of the administrators, provide data that is then distributed by the administrators via the groups in a targeted manner. In exceptional situations, this concerns targeted information about investigations, such as the recent campaign to track down a number of criminals in specific foreign cars (**Annex 8** Neighbourhood Watch, and Report Crime Anonymously). The administrators are committed to ensuring that the communities and the software and data that is used remain the property of the residents themselves. They have explicitly looked into a neighbouring, larger municipality; here the police introduced an app platform in which citizens could participate. However, this platform failed because it eventually led to fragmentation, did not result in cooperation between citizens, and because there was no sense of ownership. People only felt supported by the municipality in an administrative sense, and there was not much support in terms of expertise when it came to crime prevention. In practice, it was mainly the police who actively assisted the community in this. For example, by offering training course in various neighbourhoods about specific situations or on how to report crimes.

3. Scanning and prioritisation

- Determine whether there are (major) problems with HIC in your municipality and what the consequences are. Use the following as input:
    - Police data (portal, scan, early warning system).
    - Weigh up the levels of seriousness.
    - If necessary, make a broader assessment of the total picture of local crime in the municipality (on the basis of conversations with key people or a periodic survey among residents).

- Especially look at concentrations: Hot times – Hot places / Hot spots – Hot shots – Hot victims (population and organisations).

- Indicate roughly what should be achieved with regard to this problem by citizens/institutions/ companies, the municipality, the police and the Public Prosecutor (OM).

- Choose one or more of the cited problems (prioritisation) and analyse them in the next step (analysis).

3.1 Pay continual attention to HIC

Ambitious

The fact that addressing High Impact Crime (HIC) became a priority was already determined in 2009 *(Grapperhaus, 2019)* and a lot has been achieved since then. Nevertheless, the number of residential burglaries, armed robberies and street robberies is still considerable, and the consequences remain serious. In addition, we still see worrying concentrations in certain neighbourhoods, in hot spots, among (groups of) offenders and in some victim groups (recurrent victimisation). We also know that criminal youth groups in particular play an important role in these criminal offences. Also see the examples:

"Analyse en aanpak jeugdnetwerk" and "Aanpak hot shots *('Analysis and Tackling of a Youth Network'* **and** *'Tackling Hot Shots', Beke et al., 2013* **and** *Braga et al., 2019 respectively)*". **HIC is often** an intermediary station for budding juvenile offenders, who then progress to the serious crime circuit. The extent of the misery that drugs and associated assassinations lead to has become increasingly clear in recent years. In this case, too, Benjamin Franklin's saying applies that "an ounce of prevention is worth a pound of cure" (although at the time he was talking about fire safety).

Reason enough to keep a constant eye on local signals and occasionally step things up a notch. But when should you devote more attention to HIC?

You determine this on the basis of:

- police data on the scope of crime: how often does it occur;
- the seriousness of the crime;
- the unrest caused by HIC.

It is especially important to analyse the following concentrations: Hot times - Hot places / Hot spots - Hot shots - Hot victims.

3.2 Focus on concentrations

Crime is never neatly spread out evenly. There is a lot more crime than in other places in some areas (hot spots). Clear differences can also be seen in terms of time (hot times: hours of the day, days of the week, months of the year, seasons): there are more burglaries when it is dark outside, for instance. A comparable concentration also applies to perpetrators and victims. For example, there are multiple offenders and repeat victims: after a burglary, the chance of recurrence - including at neighbouring houses - is higher than average. We refer to this as *clustering* or the *law of concentration of crime*. Also see Knowledge Pearl 229*.

In the Netherlands too, there is a skewed distribution of problems with criminals.

- Almost 45% of violence takes place among only 10% of victims who work in the public sector. This concentration of victimisation can also be found in the business world. For example, three percent of the total number of branches within the retail sector account for more than 50% of the estimated total victimisation.

- When it comes to perpetrators, five percent of known offenders appear to be responsible for 40% of specific criminal offences.

- Nor is crime distributed evenly on a geographical basis either. There are so-called "hot places" or "hot spots". These are places, neighbourhoods and locations where crime occurs above the average amount. For example, there are certain industrial estates where (organised) crime is rampant. These are concentrated "criminal hot spots".

In short, crime is distributed unevenly. For crime analysts, this offers excellent opportunities to make analyses based on this skewed distribution of where different types of crime will occur.

* More information about sources, see the digital version at **www.prohic.nl**

It is very important to raise the alarm in areas with high concentrations of crime. This is all related to the 80/20 rule, otherwise known as the Pareto Principle. The Italian mathematician and economist Vilfredo Pareto noted in 1906 that 80% of the Italian economy is controlled by 20% of the population. This rule subsequently turned out to apply to more subjects: 80% of the outcomes or consequences are caused by 20% of the causes. Or: 80% of the output or result comes from only 20% of the input.

Crime and threats to safety are never evenly distributed, not geographically, not in time, and not even within groups of perpetrators and victims.

Identifying these concentrations of crime, and subsequently tackling them, turns out to be the most important golden law of crime science. It is precisely at hot spots/hot times that extra action must be taken. At the same time, hot shots/hot groups (frequent offenders/recidivists) and the people, households or companies that repeatedly become victims (hot victims) also deserve close attention.

3.3 The triangle decides

In the end the answer to the question 'what crimes should be tackled?' is ultimately provided by the local triangle based on an integral information analysis that looks at the nature, extent and seriousness of the local crime situation, and at HIC in particular. See sections on police data (3.5), seriousness (3.6) and a broader prioritisation (3.7).

Decisions by the triangle are preferably made on the basis of a memorandum from the police chief of the local Local Policing Unit and the municipal head of Public Order and Security (OOV). They will usually involve an analyst, operations specialist and municipal researcher in this process. The memorandum contains an opinion about the HIC situation in the municipality, scope[6], location (neighbourhoods), a timeline (years/trends) and a proposal or recommendation - to be approved by the triangle - regarding prioritisation. As in, which of the three HIC problems is given priority and in which neighbourhoods. Initial ideas about potential directions for solutions may also be included.

Following on from that, the question must be answered as to who will be involved and what initial ideas there are on potential solutions. In this respect, aspects such as the goals to be achieved, the resources to be invested (time/money) and the deadline deserve to be addressed and tested out first.

It is also useful to propose who will be the project leader (and deputy), who will be part of a small project group, and how often any progress should be reported to the triangle. Frequently this is already laid out in the IVB/IGP approach and can be made use of. The triangle also examines whether it agrees with the initial ideas about possible directions for solutions. The triangle decides on the main lines, policy choices and strategy, but not on concrete measures. The triangle leaves this aspect to the professionals and their partners.

Even though the focus is on priorities, this does not mean that non-prioritised crimes, neighbourhoods or groups no longer receive any attention.

---

[6] In terms of scale, it is not just about the absolute figures, yet if people want to compare the scale in different municipalities (e.g.: 'Do we score better/worse than our neighbours?'), then it is important to relate the absolute figure to the probability that a criminal offence may occur. The number of residential burglaries can best be compared to the number of homes.

3.4 Project Group

The triangle determines who will be the project leader and who will be part of the project group. A member of the triangle shall serve as the contact person and will be responsible for periodic reporting within the triangle.

The composition of this project group pays close attention to everything that is taking place. The choice for smart interventions is made on the grounds of good information and rational considerations. Preferably by people who are not afraid to go off the beaten track and who can work well together.

Finally, good contact with and knowledge from "above" (triangle) and "below" (execution) are important. In public administration, this is referred to as a "vital coalition".

Five conditions are essential for a vital coalition, says Dominic Schrijer (Alderman of Rotterdam, Mayor of Zwijndrecht and Commissioner for a housing corporation): a sense of urgency to tackle the problem, a shared vision about the future, scope for pioneers and people who can make connections, administrators who provide backing to pioneers and enough money and manpower *(Schrijer, 2019)*.

3.5 Police Data

[handwritten margin note: Book should be written for end Country Context]

Data Portal

Where HIC is concerned, police data offer a fairly accurate reflection of reality. Data on the number of residential burglaries, armed robberies and street robberies can be found in the police data portal that is freely accessible to everyone.

Here data can be found per criminal offence, per municipality (and even per district) and per year/month. An analysis over a number of years per municipality is therefore relatively easy to make. The portal dates back to 2012.

The Police Data Portal

https://data.politie.nl/#/Politie/nl/ is the police's data portal and contains figures on reported crimes, nuisance, police performance and police operations. Everyone can compile their own tables and graphs with this and the information can be downloaded with relative ease. The website contains statistical figures. Every table includes an explanation that shows how the figures are organised. In addition, an extensive list of definitions of the reported criminal offences is available at: www.politie.nl/algemeen/dataportaal/dataportaal-definities.html

Supplementary information that is aimed more at citizens: https://inbraakbarometer.nl/resultaat#2807 (Interpolis Insurers). The website deals exclusively with residential burglaries.

Area Scan

Many police teams carry out a periodic area scan (**Annex 10**), which depicts the local safety levels and which partly serves as the basis for the municipality's local safety plan *(Beke et al., 2008)*. Incidentally, in preparations for the decision-making process by the triangle, the municipality and public prosecutor should join the meeting that addresses the area scan and share their knowledge and information there.

The area scan identifies the hot spots, hot shots, hot groups, hot victims and hot times on the basis of systemic and practical knowledge. Attention is also paid to criminal youth groups. Based on this information, the triangle can decide what elements need to be tackled as a matter of priority.

In addition to the area scan, the Crime Anticipation System (CAS) can also be useful, especially the CAS maps (**Annex 11**). CAS is a tool for predictive policing. Most predictive policing systems are location-oriented and use the so-called near-repeat approach. This theory is based on criminological insights that suggest that there is a good chance that a crime will take place again in the same street or neighbourhood. The CAS is a tool that is available in every Local Policing Unit. Incidentally, the use of predictive policing tools, especially those that do not focus on locations but rather on individuals (perpetrators, victims), receives quite a lot of criticism (see *Gonzalez Fuster, 2020, Gstrein & Zwitter, 2020* and www.cuttingcrimeimpact.eu).

Early Warning

Every month and every week, the national police create a so-called Early Warning list containing the crime figures of the past week, month and year starting from 1 January for each municipality and each Local Policing Unit. This Early Warning list also compares the data with the same period in the previous year.

Alarm Bells

In essence, these sources and instruments always involve four so-called *alarm bell questions*:

1.

Has a type of crime risen over time?

2.

Does the municipality (or district) score higher than other comparable municipalities/neighbourhoods (or: the region/the whole country)?

3.

Does it appear to be one or several perpetrators/ offender groups or types of victims?

4.

Is there a concentration of crimes, perpetrators, victims and/or stolen items?

When using police data, strict rules apply that are laid down by the Act on General Data Protection Regulation/Personal Data Protection (AVG/Wpg) (**Annex 12**).

3.6 Weighing up the seriousness of the crime?

Probate
Impact
Murder
Shoplift

A residential burglary has a 'high impact' on residents, for example, because strangers have been rummaging in their closets and items that have emotional value have disappeared or have been broken. But can you actually measure the seriousness of a crime? Is there such a thing as a 'measure of evil'? The decision to take the seriousness of something into account (**Annex 13**) is up to you. Whoever wants to do this, could base the seriousness on the costs/damages (the harm done) and/or the severity of sentences.

In addition to making use of 'costs' and 'sentencing' as indicators for the seriousness of a crime, it is also an option to engage in discussions with experts. For example, consider making an inventory of the impressions of police officers, municipal employees (OVV) and citizens, institutions and companies. There may even be different kinds of 'experts' for each type of criminal offence. For instance, housing managers know more about residential burglaries and companies know more about armed robberies. Therefore, having a close relationship with these types of 'HIC specialists' is important. One can have conversations with these HIC specialists or make mathematical calculations, or even commission other specialists to do the math. In essence, it is about analysing the HIC problem in both a quantitative and qualitative sense.

3.7 HIC within the context of a broader prioritisation

Within the framework of the local integrated safety policy (IVP in Dutch), which has often been created in the context of the multi-year IVP, a broader prioritisation is almost always necessary. After all, a lot more criminal offences take place in a municipality than just residential burglaries, armed robberies and street robberies. Ultimately, what matters most are what forms of crime and safety threats affect citizens and institutions the most. This can vary considerably per district or neighbourhood. Accordingly, we also have to analyse other types of violence, from domestic violence to nightlife violence, theft (bicycle, car, scooter/moped, shoplifting), pickpocketing, vandalism/destruction of property, burglary of businesses, cybercrime and arson. In addition, nowadays a local approach to subversion and human trafficking are also often given priority. However, what makes the situation difficult is that the police and the justice department are much less aware of the extent of other kinds of criminal offences. This has everything to do with the 'funnel effect' (**Annex 14**) as a result of which the police and justice department generally only see the tip of the crime iceberg. Alternatively, this is also referred to as the '*dark number*'.

The broader picture of local crime becomes much clearer by not only analysing police figures, but also collecting information through other means. This is a form of 'triangulatio' (**Annex 15**). In the Netherlands, another extensive data source is the Safety Monitor (Veiligheids Monitor, VM) from Statistics Netherlands (**Annex 1**). This is a representative standard survey among a random sample of the Dutch population (65,000 people per year) in which questions are asked about cases of victimisation ('Have you been a victim of … in the past year?'), but also about not feeling safe and (dis)satisfaction with the police. Based on this annual random sample, the VM can make illustrative statements about the whole of the Netherlands and about the larger municipalities (>70,000 residents). Anyone who wants to make illustrative statements in smaller municipalities or on a neighbourhood level are more or less forced to 'participate in the VM'. This must be arranged and paid for separately.[7] On an international level, there are also so-called *victim surveys*. This enables the Dutch situation to be seen in an international perspective and makes it easier to see in which aspects the Netherlands is better or worse off. Well-known examples include the *International Crime Victim Survey* (ICVS), for which the Dutch founder Jan J. M. van Dijk was once awarded the 'Nobel Prize' for Criminology (2012)[*]. For Europe specifically, there is the research from the European Union Agency for Fundamental Rights (FRA 2014 and 2021).

Sometimes a lot more information is available locally about crime in the area in the form of local victim surveys (individuals, households, companies/institutions) and/ or additional information from Statistics Netherlands. For example, because a municipality is participating in the VM and

opts for a broader random sampling rate in the area. The Dutch footballer Johan Cruijff once said: *'You'll only actually start to see it once you realise it's there'*. This is also true for data on crime. There are many more sources of crime data in addition to police figures. Security problems in the area of subversion or cybercrime, for example, are extremely difficult to visualise on the basis of police figures alone. The same goes for many other crimes. Sometimes additional questions are asked locally about other criminal offences (or, more specifically, pertaining to some police teams) in the Safety Monitor from Statistics Netherlands. We should also explicitly refer to the ideas from the Cambridge Harm Index Consensus here (which takes the level of seriousness into account **Annex 13**).

As stated previously: for the three main forms of HIC (residential burglaries, armed robberies and street robberies), the data from the Safety Monitor are only really useful as general background information. The police have access to a lot of good information on HIC, both nationally and locally.

---

[7] The local participant can decide for themselves whether a random sample is requested at municipal level or whether it is necessary to zoom in further on districts and neighbourhoods within the municipality. If a further focus on certain districts and neighbourhoods is wanted, it is recommended to base the classification on the district and neighbourhood classification system applied by Statistics Netherlands (CBS). This classification has been determined together with the municipalities themselves and the Association of Netherlands Municipalities and is periodically updated. The local participant then determines, usually in close consultation with Statistics Netherlands or the VM research agency, which net number of respondents is preferred per (sub-)area. Next, an estimate has to be made of the gross number of individuals that should be drawn from the CBS random sample frameworks. Also see: http://www.veiligheidsmonitor.nl/Werkwijze/Steekproeftrekking.

[*] More information about sources, see the digital version at www.prohic.nl

Last but not least, it is worth remembering that safety is also - and perhaps above all - a subjective concept.[8] Or as people in America often say:

Perception is Reality.

8 Guillén-Lasierra, 2021; also see CCI-tool 'Perception matters': www.cuttingcrimeimpact.eu/imagem/Perception%20 Matters.pdf

3.8 Summary

When you pay more attention to HIC, you make decisions based on the following questions:

• How often does it occur? • How serious is it? • What type of unrest is caused?

Crime is not spread evenly in terms of time/location/people. In identifying and **prioritising** crime, take into account to what extent there are:

• Hot times • Hot places/Hot spots • Hot shots/Hot groups • Hot victims

Based on the integral data analysis that has been made, the local triangle determines what types of crime are to be tackled. The triangle decides on the main lines, policy choices and strategy, yet not on concrete measures. For the latter, they appoint a project group to form an 'vital coalition'.

There are various types of police data than can help with scanning and prioritising:

• Data portal (everyone) • Area Scan & CAS (police) • Early Warning (police)

These tools help answer questions about:

• Increases over time • Similar municipalities/neighbourhoods • Type of perpetrator(s)/victim(s) • Concentration of crimes/offender(s)/victim(s)/stolen goods

> *Please note! When using police data, strict regulations apply that are legally laid down in the **Police Data Act and the GDPR**.*

If someone wants to take into account the seriousness of a crime, then they can make sure that the costs/damages and/or the punishments are made known. In essence, it is about analysing the HIC problem in both a quantitative and qualitative sense.

A broader consideration is required within the framework of the local integrated safety policy. By not only looking at police figures, a broader picture of local crimes becomes much sharper and clearer. This is a form of "triangulation". For example, think of:

• The Safety Monitor (VeiligheidsMonitor) from Statistics Netherlands • Local (victim) surveys

Check/Fill in

Before proceeding, please first check ...

1. What triangle are we referring to? Who is part of it?

2. Is there a HIC project group and if so, who is part of it?

☐ Yes ☐ No

3. Has the triangle and project group (or others) established a multi-year policy with regard to HIC? For example, in the context of a broader assessment of the total picture of local crime in the municipality

☐ Yes ☐ No

4. Have any (major) problems with HIC been identified in your municipality? Briefly describe in keywords:

☐ Yes ☐ No

5. What are the consequences of these? Briefly describe in keywords:

6. In determining this, was use made of

- police data;
- data portal information;
- a scan;
- the early warning system.

☐ Yes ☐ No

```



```

7. Has the seriousness of the HIC offences been weighed up?
If so, briefly describe this in key words:

☐ Yes ☐ No

```



```

8. Is there a general indication of what should be achieved with respect to this problem?
If yes, briefly describe this in terms of general goals:

☐ Yes ☐ No

```



```

9. On the basis of sound and reliable data, have any priorities been established together with the parties mentioned (how do we tackle the problem together)? ☐ Yes ☐ No Which priorities?

```



```

10. Has this - including the creation of a project group - been clearly communicated to all those involved and the residents and organisations in the municipality (or the relevant district/area)?

☐ Yes ☐ No

```



```

Tackling Armed Robberies

History of origin

In 2009, the Dutch Minister of Justice Ernst Hirsch Ballin set up the Armed Robberies Task Force. The Task Force was appointed due to a worrying increase in the number of armed robberies in the Netherlands. Ever since 2009, there has been a decline in the number of armed robberies. Whereas there were 3,065 armed robberies in 2009, this number fell to 1,180 in 2019. That is a decline of 62%.

Working Method of the Armed Robberies Task Force

The Armed Robberies Task Force no longer only focuses on armed robberies, but also on other High Impact Crime, such as street robberies and ram-raids and explosives used in e.g., safe-cracking. It is a national platform in which the Public Prosecutor, the police, the Ministry of Justice and Security, municipalities and the business community are all represented.

The members of the Armed Robberies Task Force each represent an organisation and a constituency that benefits from an integrated approach to HIC. The Dutch Banking Association recently joined the Task Force on the recommendation of the Ministry of Justice and Security. The Task Force has research carried out that analyses the problems related to certain themes and, on the basis of this, makes recommendations about measures that should be taken. For example, in 2010, the Task Force commissioned an analysis of the problems behind the rise in armed robberies and the opportunities for tackling them *(Rovers et al., 2010)*. Based on this research, the Task Force came up with an action programme in 2011 to reduce the number of armed robberies.

The Task Force also collects best practices and comes up with and implements innovative measures itself. Examples of this include the implementation of the now widely recognised behavioural intervention "Only you determine who you are"[9] or the development of the Business Security Warranty (Keurmerk Veilig Ondernemen, KVO)[10] in which the Armed Robberies Task Force played an important role. A final, but very important task is to engender a sense of urgency and commitment among the various parties involved. Only if the sense of urgency is taken seriously and there is a commitment to tackling problems, can problems be properly addressed.

Research and recommendations

In 2016, the Task Force commissioned Cyrille Fijnaut and Ben Rovers to conduct research into how armed robberies are addressed along with a look ahead to the future *(Fijnaut & Rovers, 2016)*. What successes have been achieved by which measures? The Task Force also expressed the desire to look at the sustainability of the measures taken, so that after initial successes they are not lost due to a slackening of focus. This research showed, among other things, that sustained attention and investment in a good cooperation of the parties involved does pay off, although reactively setting up of temporary Task Forces or project groups does not lead to effective results in most cases.

Furthermore, it appeared that perpetrators of armed robberies often can still be influenced in their behaviour. These perpetrators are referred to as *The Sad* because armed robberies are a way for them to escape the problems they experience in everyday life. This approach of dealing with their background problems works well with this group. *The Bad*, on the other hand, is a group that is keen to commit crime, whereby other problems are not directly impacting their behaviour. In these cases, it has been found that stricter punishment leads to better results. Promoting prevention measures in the business community also seems to be a worthwhile measure. Also, a focus by the police and the Public Prosecution Service (setting up a team, for example) can greatly benefit criminal investigation practices. This research is an excellent example of how the Armed Robberies Task Force can make well-founded recommendations on a national and local level to very different sectors within society (municipalities, business, police, etc.).

---

[9] www.alleenjijbepaalt.nl/over-ajb

[10] hetccv.nl/keurmerken/expert/keurmerk-veilig-ondernemen/

Recent developments

In 2018, there was (once again) a rise in the number of armed robberies. The Task Force refers in particular to a significant increase in the number of armed robberies on takeaway meal deliverers. There was also an increase in the number of armed robberies on shopkeepers. It is unclear whether this is a break in the trend, but it does show that all parties still need to pay attention to these issues. The number of armed robberies of residential homes is decreasing slightly, as is the number of explosives used in e.g., safe-cracking and ram-raids.

Local approach in Rotterdam

In 2013, the municipality of Rotterdam launched the 2014-2018 Safety Programme as part of the *#veilig010* project. This programme presented the plans for improving safety levels and feelings of safety for the following four years. The plan included many of the recommendations proposed by the Armed Robberies Task Force. One important recommendation was crime prevention on the front line. This plays a particularly important role within the Safety Programme. For example, frequent offenders are closely monitored. Attention is also paid to tackling background problems that may have driven criminals to commit an offence. Helping brothers and sisters is also mentioned in the programme. This is a prime example of crime prevention rather than punishment. Other preventive measures by the Task Force were also included in the programme. For instance, there is a strong commitment to placing cameras at businesses where the police can keep an eye on things. This was a direct recommendation from the Task Force. Various partners who were part of the Task Force were also included in Rotterdam's approach to HIC. Housing corporations were involved in burglary prevention in homes, for one thing.

In 2018, the Municipality of Rotterdam presented the new Safety Programme 2018-2023. This included an overview of the successes that have already been booked. The document shows that the number of armed robberies has declined by 43% since 2012. Other HIC, such as street robberies (muggings) and residential burglaries, have also fallen sharply. It is clear that the municipality of Rotterdam is paying close attention to the recommendations made by the Armed Robberies Task Force and is achieving considerable success by doing so.

4. Analysis

What exactly do we know about the problem that is to be tackled (location/time/ perpetrators/victims, nature/ scope/development) and who is involved? Which parties are already tackling the problem and what are they doing?

How/why has the problem arisen (cause/effect): what causes what?

4.1 Mapping out problems in more detail

In the previous step, the triangle has made the decision to tackle one, two or all three HIC problems. The triangle also gave priority to specific areas or neighbourhoods and/or perpetrator or victim groups. The next step entails a careful analysis of what exactly the HIC problem is, who is causing it (where and when), who the victim is (where and when) and which institutions (from the municipality, police, Public Prosecution Servicer or other action-takers/stakeholders) are already doing something about it and/or could do more about it. The police and municipality may (preferably jointly) carry out this type of analysis and also involve residents and other local stakeholders. Outsourcing to external parties, such as research agencies or universities, is sometimes recommended if more (scientific) expertise and experience are required, or if there are simply no researchers or analysists available. The project group may act as a supervisory committee for an external analysis.

For further analysis, it is also advisable to use triangulation (**Annex 15**): multiple sources of information and methods to get a picture of the underlying causes of the problem.

Various methods can be used to give structure to the analysis. We will discuss two of these:

• the crime triangle;

• the seven Golden Ws (who, what, where, when, why, with what, and in what way).

4.2 Crime Triangle

The crime triangle (also known as the safety triangle) appears to be useful in daily practice as a starting point for tackling the problem of crime in an integrated and targeted manner together with partners and citizens.

The triangle[11] identifies the three most important factors for crime: there must be one or more motivated perpetrators and one or more vulnerable victims who meet each other at a time and in a location where there is hardly any surveillance/oversight, if at all (crime scene/situation).

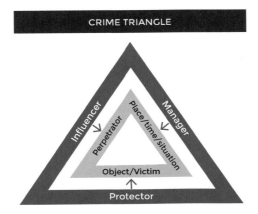

In fact, the crime triangle actually consists of two triangles. In the inner triangle, the emphasis is on analysis: what exactly is going on with regard to this crime? Where does it take place and who are the perpetrator(s) and victim(s)? The outer triangle focuses more on the question of who could contribute to the approach. This triangle directly relates to the measures taken: who can do something?

---

[11] Source of the figures in English: https://popcenter.asu.edu/content/problem-analysis-triangle-0. Also see in Dutch p. 28 of: https://popcenter.asu.edu/sites/default/files/library/reading/PDFs/60steps_dutch.pdf.

Example of a theft/mugging
Inside a parking garage

In this example, we assume the following set of data that have emerged from a municipal joint survey (Annex 16).

The location/situation concerns a public parking garage (name/address and exact details known) where outsiders have easy access. It is a fairly old parking garage belonging to a large apartment complex. Drug addicts and homeless people use dark corners of the garage to hide, use or deal drugs and to sleep. They leave their used needles and other drug-related paraphernalia in the parking garage and also appear to be responsible for many of the thefts from motor vehicles. But muggings also take place, mainly in the evenings.

There is no entrance control for the parking garage and the garage has previously been described as easily accessible for outsiders.

As such: Theft from cars and muggings:
1st /inner triangle

Perpetrators	Drugs users
Location/Situation/ Time	Public parking garage (evening)
Object/Victim	Cars belonging to parkers and the parkers themselves

More detailed information is also considered, such as the number of thefts and muggings (including modus operandi, times, exact locations, stolen items) and information about the suspected perpetrators (number of people, known to the police/others).

For potential measures, we first look at the second/outer triangle:

Theft from cars and muggings:
1st /triangle and 2nd /outer triangle

Perpetrator	Drugs users
Location/Situation/Time	Public parking garage
Object/Victim	Cars belonging to parkers and the parkers themselves

Influencer	City name
Manager	Housing corporation XX
Protector	The parkers themselves (theft of valuables from a car), additional protection through lighting, entrance control, CCTV and immediate intervention in the event of foul play

Recommendations/approach

What is immediately apparent is that not much, if anything, is known about the perpetrators. Who or what could induce them to change their behaviour? Finding this out requires discussions with both the users themselves and care providers (municipal health services, carers, local drug experts).

We know the parking garage manager and are able to roughly indicate what this manager could do as a protector. For example, making entrance control mandatory for using the parking garage, a major refurbishment, better lighting, surveillance and cameras. And the people who park their cars can do something too: make sure that they do not leave any valuables in their cars. The best approach seems to be to take various measures at the same time, which also involves the perpetrators by arranging good alternative shelter for and with them.

Tips

- **Similar study case (from 2009):** www.dsp-groep.nl/wp-content/uploads/18kkalkgar_Advies_sociale_veiligheid_parkeergarage_Karperton.pdf

- **One more:** www.vexpan.nl/wp-content/uploads/2015/11/Vexpansie3-veiligh.-in-P-garages.pdf

- **International Information** https://popcenter.asu.edu/content/thefts-and-cars-parking-facilities-references

Go to/Fill in for "your problem"

Perpetrator	//fill in//

Location/Situation/Time	,,

Object/Victim	,,

Influencer	//fill in//

Manager	,,

Protector	,,

4.3 Golden Ws

This approach is similar to the crime triangle, but depending on the situation, sometimes the triangle is more effective and other times the Golden Ws are. This simple analysis instrument has been used by journalists and police officers for several decades. In journalistic circles, it is also sometimes referred to as the Five Ws + H: Who? What? Where? When? Why? And How?. In policing circles, it is simply referred to as the **Golden Ws: who, what, where, when, why, with what** and **in what way**.

Who is involved: perpetrators, victims and (potential) witnesses? An individual, or groups? More information about this can be found in Knowledge Pearl 37[*], Knowledge Pearl 16[*], Knowledge Pearl 18[*], Knowledge Pearl 19[*] and Knowledge Pearl 230[*] (all of which – as in many more - can be found on www.ProHIC.nl).

What happened: what criminal offence took place and how did it take place? For example, think about the preparation, planning and selection of a target, risk assessment, the actual crime itself (burglaries/armed robberies/street robberies), removal/exit/escape, fencing/selling on stolen goods. In cases of burglaries and armed robberies, think about the world-famous Dutch PCCE-ALRE theory. ALRE stands for: ALarm/ALert and Response/REact.

PCCE stands for the phases that make up a crime like a burglary or armed robbery:

- Planning (target selection, scoping out the scene beforehand, stolen goods, and risk assessment)
- Committing the actual crime: the burglary or armed robbery
- Collecting the stolen goods
- Exit/escape

For example, a burglar breaking into homes would prefer to have two escape routes (e.g., after breaking in through the kitchen door at the back, he walks out the front door and leaves it open) and prefers not to stay too long (no more than 10 minutes) stealing stuff. The PCCE steps have a time sequence and the ALRE - the alarm/alert and response/react - must be in line with this. For burglaries, also see Knowledge Pearl 227*.

Where does the crime take place? Demarcate the area where HIC occurs. This can be in specific places throughout the whole municipality, but also in a particular district or neighbourhood. A map can often help with this (also see the hot spot analysis by the police; **Annex 10**). More information can be found in Knowledge Pearl 39*, Knowledge Pearl 15* en Knowledge Pearl 229*.

When does it take place? Year(s), month(s), week(s), day(s), hour(s). Be aware that a lot of data is not very precise. The exact time of a residential burglary is often not entirely clear ("it occurred sometime during the weekend").

Why did the perpetrators act in a particular way? The essence of the "why" is that the perpetrators are familiar with the location and the loot. It then comes down to "a lot of loot" and "little risk" (risk-reward).

What is used to commit the crime? A weapon? A large screwdriver (still commonly used in home burglaries)?

in What way do the perpetrators act: the modus operandi (MO).

* More information about sources, see the digital version at **www.prohic.nl**

An example of the application of the **Ws**

We have already seen that there are many hundreds of measures and projects aimed at tackling HIC. Yet it is important to realise that a local approach often emerges very clearly from a thorough analysis. For example, let's say that locally, we see that home burglaries mainly take place in the Vogelbuurt, a neighbourhood full of 1960s single-family homes with fire lanes (as in the photos opposite) and that the seven Golden Ws are responded to by the police and the municipality as follows.

Who according to the police, quite a few frequent repeat offenders live in the adjacent Bloemenbuurt and a certain youth group seems to be particularly active in the Vogelbuurt.

What thefts/break-ins in single-family homes from the Eigen Huis housing corporation. Minor stolen goods each time, small, easily sellable items.[12]

Where in the Vogelbuurt (a close-knit working-class neighbourhood with a lot of social control), at the rear of the houses.

When especially after dark.

---

[12] Ronald Clarke (1999) talks about 'hot products' which are CRAVED: Concealable, Removable, Available, Valuable, Enjoyable, and Disposable.

Why theft of small items that are easy to carry (money, banks cards, jewellery, etc).

in What way modus operandi = use of a break-in tool to jimmy open the top window at the back of the kitchen. Crawling inside (must be a lean athletic type), opening the back door of the kitchen and stealing things from the house (ground floor only).

In such a case, the approach is obvious, although it depends on the available options. If the police have the time and energy and the Public Prosecutor gives priority to catching/punishing these types of perpetrators, an attempt can be made to catch them in the act *(Van Dijk et al., 2013)*. At the same time, they may also collaborate more closely with potential victims by asking them to leave the lights on, keeping an eye on neighbours' homes when they are away or calling the police in case of any suspicious situations.

Lastly, preventive measures can also be taken on a situational basis: have the housing corporation improve the burglar-proof features at the rear of these houses, install lighting, secure the back alleys, etc. (see the various requirements from the Police Label Safe and Secure Housing).

On the basis of a good but quick analysis of the Golden Ws, the step to targeted effective action is often not so big. We also see that the approach is to a large extent - as it were "independent" of the analysis - guided by the feasibility of the action: who can do what. In other words, if the police have a lack of capacity, it is important to start taking more 'victim-oriented' and 'location-oriented' measures, instead of 'perpetrator-oriented' measures. The police then spot signals and give advice ('here is something going on and these are the facts concerning the seven Golden Ws).

4.4 Information Sources

The information needed to be able to answer the Crime Triangle and Golden W questions is varied, coming from different sources and collected with a variety of methods and techniques. Often, a lot of information is already available from the scanning and prioritisation phase (Chapter 3). The following are some examples of sources.

4.4.1 Numerical/Quantitative

- Area scan (**Annex 10**) and CAS maps (**Annex 11**). Ask for a good and recent hot spot map from the police for the types of crime/HIC (and neighbourhood) they are targeting.

- Police data. In addition to the hot spot analyses already mentioned, the police often conduct problem-oriented perpetrator group analyses, whereby offenders can be better identified. An example of such an analysis by the Beresteinlaan police station in The Hague can be found in **Annex 17**. Also see *Ferwerda and Van Ham, 2015* and the *Wegwijzer jeugd en veiligheid (Youth and Safety Pointer)*.

- The work methods (Modus Operandi [13]) of the perpetrators could also be uncovered on the basis of police data or information from other institutions (such as housing associations in the event of residential burglaries). For example, how exactly did the perpetrator proceed? Analysis of these data may reveal certain patterns.

- Local research: is there any local research available into home burglaries, street robberies or armed robberies? Yes/No. If so, what ......

[13] For example, see the national Modus Operandi study on residential burglaries: https://hetccv.nl/onderwerpen/woninginbraak/documenten/hoe-doen-ze-het-toch-modus-operandi-woninginbraak/ (a replication of comparable research done in The Netherlands 1991).

Important tips

- **KIS.** Keep It Simple. Some of these analyses may involve months of research and that is not really the intention.

- The scale seems fairly simple to determine: based on the number of police reports, but be aware that any comparison should always relate to the probability of a crime occurring. The number of home burglaries in Amsterdam is obviously much higher than in Bronckhorst. But it is about the risk of burglary. The number of home burglaries as a percentage of the total number of homes (or as a proxy, the number of households) in a municipality. Or the number of ram-raids as a percentage of the total number of ATMs in the municipality (or, if unknown, a proxy as a 'number of residents').

- A warning when using data: be careful, because personally identifiable data may not, or rarely, be shared (WPG/AVG - Act on Police Data/GDPR). In many cases, this is not necessary either. Always make sure the data are not personally identifiable (anonymised) before sharing them with others (see **Annex 12**).

4.4.2 Qualitative

- **Conversations**: take a look around and consider who, in addition to experts at the police and municipality, has knowledge of current HIC problems. For example, what about housing corporations, residents/neighbourhood associations or local insurance agents where home burglaries are concerned? Or asking the chair of a business association about armed robberies? Information from the special investigating officers (BOAs)? A youth worker who knows more about criminal groups? This information also tells us who the active players are in HIC field, what they do, and what they know. A few conversations often yields plenty of useful information that can help flesh out the Crime Triangle or the Golden Ws in more detail.

- **Joint surveys**: Go on a walk with other involved parties and observe what's going on In the Netherlands, walking around together and observing an area (joint surveys) has been common practice for a very long time

(Luten, 2008). It involves visiting a problem area and determining what is going well and what can be improved. This kind of joint survey is often carried out by a group of local residents, sometimes together with people from the municipality (from councillors to lighting experts). When it concerns social safety, these joint surveys are carried out during the day, but also after dark and at dawn and dusk. There are countless forms of joint surveys, but in essence, a group walks around and observes everything with a very specific focus.

When it comes to HIC, it is also worthwhile looking around as if you were a burglar or an armed robber (!) or a mugger. What opportunities do you see? Try and look from the perspective of the perpetrator. Also see Knowledge Pearl 29*. More ideas about joint surveys can be found in **Annex 16**.

- **Forgotten groups**: there are also other groups that do not readily come to mind. Children/young people often know more than you may think. For example, about the possession of weapons, suspicious areas, violence and victims that are not as well known.

  However children do require a completely different approach. Through the use of drawings or stories, for example. There are very good examples from Central and South America - where violence is endemic. Here is an example from Mexico: →

'Bienvenidos a la escuela de armas' by Rau and Neri 2019 and Rau 2021

Besides children and young people, there are plenty of other 'hidden' groups. Also consider refugees who are often pointed to as potential perpetrators of HIC, but who are more likely to be disproportionate victims of HIC *(Peeck et al., 2018)*.

- **Crime scripts**: a crime script can be created for every type of crime. This involves mapping out the different phases or scenes. These phases describe what has to happen in order for the criminal offence to eventually take place. For a residential burglary, for instance, the perpetrator has to pick out the best neighbourhood and house to burgle, break into the house (from which side?), determine which (valuable) items to take, escape from the house, sell the stolen goods on, etc. Also see the PCCE-ALRE theory from 4.3.

Every phase requires one or more people to fill certain roles. Closer examination of the various components in these phases can provide insight into the problem and perhaps offer possibilities for a solution or a course of action.

4.4.3 Other useful methods and techniques for research

In the context of the EU project Cutting Crime Impact (CCI), ten simple research methods and techniques have also been summarised in English on separate flashcards (for example: observation, interview, process-mapping, focus group journaling, stakeholder mapping) (see www.ProHIC.nl).

4.4.4 Conclusion

To conclude, here are a few things to consider when looking for information:

- What do we already know about the problem to be tackled (location/time/perpetrators/victims, nature/scope/development) and who are involved? Consider using instruments such as the crime triangle and the Golden Ws.

- Who is already doing something about it and what are they doing? Consult them for more information.

- Information is almost always available in abundance. Make decisions based on the following criteria. The information must:
  De informatie moet:
  - be used for further determining which measures should be taken;
  - be reliable, valid and up to date;
  - preferably be easily and cheaply available;
  - not be traceable to individual persons (Act on Police Data/GDPR, **Annex 12**).

- Remember the section on triangulation: multiple sources, different data and different analysts. Therefore, as the police and the municipality, work together with others. But here too, it is important to keep an overview; too much information and too many people involved will not benefit either the effectiveness or the efficiency. Limit yourself to a maximum of five sources of information and other people. KIS. Keep It Simple.

4.5 Summary

By using multiple sources (triangulation), the police and municipality are able to make a careful analysis, preferably together with citizens, companies and organisations. Two methods have been highlighted:

The (double) crime triangle

- Victim ⟷ Protector
- Perpetrator ⟷ Influencer
- Location ⟷ Manager

- Who • What • Where • When • Why • With what • What way

___

You can use the information that has already been gathered from the scanning and prioritisation process to supplement these methods, and complement these further with both quantitative and qualitative information. Examples include:

- Police data • Joint surveys • Conversations • Crime scripting

Other useful research methods are available through the CCI project. Furthermore, it is important to find out:

- What knowledge is currently available • Who are currently tackling the problem • What information is available • Triangulation

Police Label Safe and Secure Housing Alkmaar

History of origin

The Dutch government memorandum on Society and Crime (Samenleving en Criminaliteit, SeC, 1985) was based heavily on the previous interim report presented by the commission on petty crime, which was chaired by Hein Roethof. The memorandum called for more attention to be paid to the design of the built-up environment as a measure to prevent crime:

> 66 *The built-up environment should, in terms of planning and architectural features be planned and designed in such a way that on the one hand, it does not unnecessarily hamper the monitoring of young people in particular, and on the other hand it does not unnecessarily make it easier to commit thefts and the like.* 99 (SeC, 1985).

Spatial planning, urban planning and architecture were suddenly presented as the way to tackle residential burglaries. This is referred to as 'Crime Prevention through Environmental Design' abroad (www.CPTED.net).

In the Netherlands, the term Safe Design and Management ('Veilig Ontwerp en Beheer' was coined; www.SVOB.nl and Luten, 2008). At the time, some police officers were already involved in consulting project developers,[14] municipalities and housing corporations in the area of Safe Design and Management, but their advice was often seen as non-obligatory and was sometimes even ignored completely. With the roll-out of *Secured by Design* by the British police, more attention was paid to the ways in which homes, buildings and neighbourhoods in the Netherlands as well could be made safer through the use of smart spatial planning *(Korthals Altes et al, 1993)*. In 1994, a pilot took place for the **Dutch Police Label Safe and Secure Housing**, which focused on the development of new buildings and neighbourhoods. In 1995, this was expanded by also working further on areas that were already in existence. Another year later, in 1996, the project was rolled out nationwide.

Integrated approach

An important aspect of the Police Label is that it involves an integrated approach. This means that not only a specific home and how it can be protected against burglary is analysed, but an entire neighbourhood or even the building in which the home is located. Various partners in the design and construction process, such as urban planners, (landscape) architects, project developers, housing corporations, suppliers of wall elements, etc. work intensively with municipalities on new construction projects to reduce the chances of home burglaries taking place and to increase the sense of social safety. This involves going from working on a macro to a micro level so as to make neighbourhoods, buildings and homes safer against break-ins.

For example, for a new residential area, first the urban planning and design of the neighbourhood is analysed, followed by the public space, layout, the buildings themselves (e.g. apartment buildings/apartment blocks) and finally the burglar-proof state of the buildings. On each of these levels, attention is paid to the way in which design can contribute to the security of the area. There is a checklist for each level that includes both requirements and recommendations with regard to how design can contribute to safety levels. This form of integrated working pays off, which is apparent from the significant reduction in the risk of residential burglary in the Netherlands *(Nauta, 2004 and Van Ours & Vollaard, 2011)*.

[14] https://www.politiekeurmerk.nl/2020/06/22/25-jaar-politiekeurmerk-veilig-wonen/#:~:text=Het%20 ontstaan%20van%20het%20Politiekeurmerk,zijn%20op%20criminaliteit%20zoals%20woninginbraken.

■■■ Case Vroornermeer

In the Netherlands, numerous new construction projects are being developed according to the guidelines and requirements from the Police Label Safe and Secure Housing. An example of this is the Vroonermeer-Zuid district in Alkmaar. This district was developed from 2000 to 2005 with a total of 1,230 homes. Three quarters are owner-occupied homes and the other quarter are rental homes. Particular attention was paid to safe design at each of the levels described above. For example, in the design of the district, the access points to the district, the location of public space and certain housing types have been considered. Lighting was an important focal point in the public spaces.

Research has shown that improved lighting can lead to a 20% reduction in criminal activity *(Farrington & Welsh, 2002)*.

Facilities for young residents, such as playgrounds, have also been strategically placed so that they are clearly visible from surrounding homes. This may lead to increased social control and thus a limitation of the risk of criminal activities or nuisance incidents.

The layout of the back pathways through which people - and the fire service - can access backyards has also been cleverly designed to improve social safety and to not look attractive to potential criminals. In residential buildings, windows have been strategically placed so that social control by local residents can be increased, and home invasion-limiting measures have also been built in. The houses are also equipped with burglary-proof windows and doors that meet the regular requirements on burglary resistance where building standards are concerned (NEN standards referred to in the building decree).[15]

■■■ Results

Generally speaking, Police Label Safe and Secure Housing has contributed to a significant reduction in the number of successful residential burglaries *(Jongejan & Woldendorp, 2013)*.

To date, more than 1,000 new construction projects have been developed according to the recommendations and requirements of the Police Label

[15] Also see: https://rijksoverheid.bouwbesluit.com/Inhoud/docs/norm/nen5096-2012/4.

Safe and Secure Housing and 702,289 certificates have been issued to individual homes throughout the Netherlands *(Jongejan, 2020)*.

For individual homes that have received the certificate, the burglary risk is **80%** lower, and for homes that have been developed in the new construction projects in accordance with the requirements and recommendations of the **Police Label Safe and Secure Housing**, this is even **95%** lower.

This is also clearly evident in the Vroonermeer-Zuid district. For example, no home in this district was broken into in 2011 and the figures for vandalism, assault and theft from vehicles are also significantly lower than both the average in the Netherlands and the average in **Alkmaar** *(Lopez et al., 2013)*. The Police Label Safe and Secure Housing is not only focused on reducing the risk of residential burgalries, but also about the entire security of neighbourhoods and homes, including fire safety and lighting in and around homes. One final advantage of the Police Label is that it is possible to get a discount on home insurance from various insurers.

A problem-oriented approach to High Impact Crime

ProHIC Book of Basics

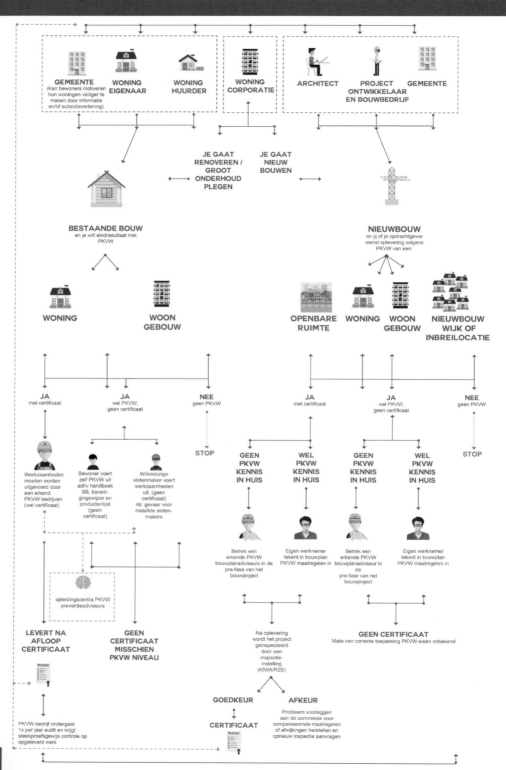

5. Action Plan

- Together with all the stakeholders involved, formulate what you want to achieve with respect to the problem, which measures are feasible in order to solve/reduce the problem and then adopt the most viable set of measures.

- Why and how could (each of) the measures work? Always give a short description and justification of the expected effect. Also look at what others (domestic/abroad) have already done/tried.

- Draw up an action plan together that contains a description of the problem, demarcation and approach (goals/ measures/planning/stakeholders/ resources) as well as the evaluation plan.

5.1 Setting goals

As the municipality, police and Public Prosecutor, it is best to determine the concrete goals in close collaboration with citizens and companies/institutions: we all want to reduce the HIC problems. Not only reduce in terms of numbers, but also reduce in terms of damage inflicted and/or reduce in terms of other social impacts (e.g., not feeling safe and dissatisfaction amongst citizens). Using the HIC problems that have been identified as a basis, sit down together and decide what needs to be achieved within a specified period of time. Try to make this as concrete as possible. For example, the aim is to go from ten armed robberies per year to a maximum of five per year (or preferably less), with a maximum damage of € xxx.

5.1.1 Goal-resources chain

Ideally, a goal-resources chain should be present. Here, a main goal, formulated in more general terms, if need be, is at the top followed by several sub-goals. The measures/resources are then listed for each sub-goal. An example of a goal-resources chain - sometimes also referred to as a goal tree - is included below. Just like a real tree, it can have an endless number of branches. In this example, the focus is on residential burglaries in which more physical types of safety (see also the example from the Police Label Safe and Secure Housing) and the chance of catching perpetrators are detailed as goals.

Example of a goal tree

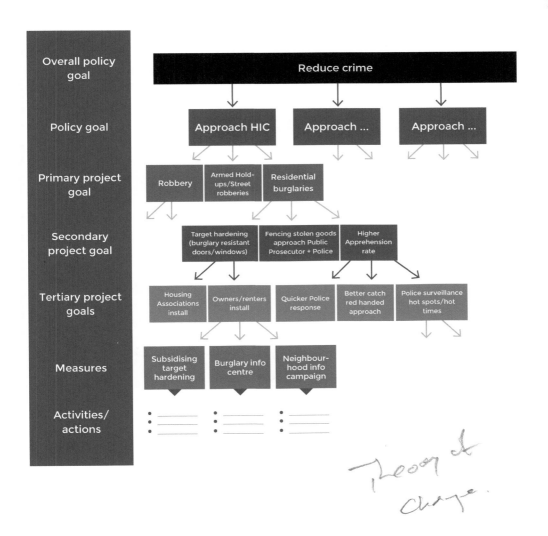

After viewing this example, it is useful to take a look at your own situation.

Check/Fill in: create your own goal-resources chain for your specific problem.

Following this example, it may be useful to create a goal-resources chain for your own situation. Software is available for this, but it is often much more convenient to work (together!) with sticky notes on the wall of the project group room.

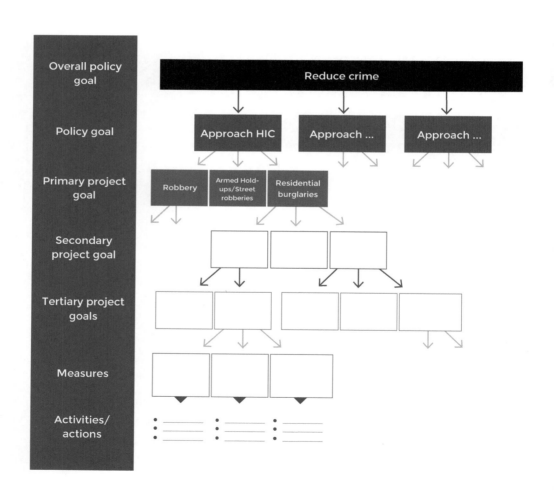

5.1.2 How SMART do you want it to be (and how SMART can you make it?)

Many books and articles about formulating and setting goals use the so-called SMART concept. SMART stands for Specific, Measurable, Achievable, Realistic and Timely (Benders, 2020). This concept is especially useful for charting and following a clear course together and to be able to properly evaluate the process and impact at a later stage. SMART may seem simple (and you should definitely try it), but in practice it is sometimes more difficult to realise than expected. Especially if there are several stakeholders involved.

If there isn't a goal, you can't score (or miss):

66 A standard outcome of practically every police evaluation, and every report by The Netherlands Court of Audit, is that it is difficult to assess policy because the goals/objectives of the policy have not been explicity formulated. And if there isn't a goal, you can't score (or miss). Neither can you improve your policy in a well-thought-out way.

Is the formulation of goals sometimes overlooked? Is it down to civil servant incompetence? No, of course not, it is down to policy. The policy is not to make any goals explicit. The reason for this is self-preservation. A minister can get into (political) problems if it turns out that certain goals have not been achieved. Therefore it is better not to have any at all, or only to have them written down in such an abstract way that they can do no harm. 99

(Kalshoven, 2021).

Wim Deetman – tried and tested Politician (House of Representatives, Minister, Mayor of The Hague, Council of State):

> *The goals set by politicians are often vague and inoperable. From these goals, it is impossible to discern clear paths in order to achieve them.*
>
> *The goals accepted by politicians are sometimes not the 'real' intentions; hence the problem of a 'hidden agenda'. Completely different, hidden goals may be the real drivers of political behaviour.*
>
> *There are more different and often conflicting goals that play a role. A clear common goal is lacking. Not only are there more roads to Rome, but also more destinations.*
>
> *Goals change over time. By the time a problem is solved, the problem definition has changed and the next problem needs to be tackled. Solving that one problem (may not) eliminate the other one.*

(Deetman, 1988, p. 30)

A recent evaluation of innovative teams working in the field of criminal investigation and prosecution within the police in The Netherlands, the Q-teams, shows that not so much has changed in the past thirty years.

> *The key question behind this research is whether Q-teams can be called a success or not. To begin with, this question can only be answered per team and therefore at a level per unit. As mentioned, there are major differences between the teams, also in the goals that they set for themselves. These goals are often not very precise and therefore difficult to measure. The context also differs greatly per Q-team. This makes it difficult, if not impossible, to make an unambiguous statement about whether Q-teams are a success.*

(Van Egmond et al., 2020, p. 113)

The same evaluation also shows that targets are sometimes adjusted in the interim.

In short: try to formulate goals in a SMART way and record the process, but do not be surprised if someone suddenly turns out to throw a spanner in the works, or if the formulated SMART goals appear to change in the interim, either because it is clearly a more efficient approach or simply because it is more politically appropriate.

Sometimes, however, there are also positive exceptions:

In Gouda the goal was to reduce the burglary risk from twenty burglaries per 1,000 homes (2016) to the unit average of eight burglaries per 1,000 homes (2019). Although this proved to be a fairly ambitious target, it was eventually achieved. In 2019, the burglary risk was indeed 8/1,000. Both the police and municipality were extremely satisfied with the result. The team leader sent an email stating the following:

 We are proud that team Gouda is named in the annual report of the Hague unit as THE example of how to tackle residential burglaries. Things were quite different in the past... We have had this focused approach in the Goverwelle district studied by a research agency and we want to present that report to the board in a few months' time. "

The mayor has responded very enthusiastically:

"Keep up the great work!"

5.2 Determining measures

In determining these measures, the key question is which measures will enable the specified goals to be achieved. Always answer the following question in advance: 'why and how could this measure work?' (= contribute to achieving the goal). The goal-resources chain (see 5.1.1) can be a useful instrument in this regard.

5.2.1 Evidence based

It is important to identify measures that have proven their worth in practice. These measures are often given the designation 'evidence-based' or 'evidenced-informed'.

From the Movisie website: *'There are major (www. movisie.nl/artikel/evidence-based-werken-geen-keurslijf) misconceptions about evidence-based approaches'*, explains **Renske van der Zwet**, researcher at the Movisie knowledge institute. The biggest misconception is that these are proven effective interventions', according to **Van der Zwet.** *'Evidence-based practice is not working with effective interventions, but rather a matter of a professional weighing up the pros and cons.. You look at the needs of the client, you consult your own expertise regarding the request for help and then you seek out scientific knowledge about the problem'.* **This is one of the reasons why the**

somewhat more relative term 'evidence-informed' is often used instead of 'evidence based'.

The last step, the search for research and scientific knowledge, is not often taken and for that reason, evidence-based work methods are not widespread among professionals. Van der Zwet received her PhD in November 2018 for research into this: *'Implementing evidence-based practice in social work: a shared responsibility'*. As the title of her dissertation indicates, not only the professional has a responsibility to use scientific knowledge in their work. *'It is also the responsibility of staff and management to support their public sector professionals in using scientific knowledge.'*

These kind of 'proofs' of what works and what doesn't also require the approach to be fully documented and evaluated. Hence the emphasis we place on conducting a good evaluation. To this day, this still happens very rarely, which is why, for example, the Centre for Crime Prevention and Security (CCV) lists 300 HIC approaches on its website. Even though it is only infrequently known whether or not an approach actually works or not. The Knowledge Pearls available on the website www.ProHIC.nl provide answers here. Also see the influential report Preventing crime: **What Works, What Doesn't, What's Promising** *(Sherman et al., 1998).*

Nevertheless, a warning is appropriate here too. Time and place are almost always linked to proven effectiveness. What is effective in the United States, for example, may not be effective in a Dutch municipality. **Context matters!** Therefore, always look at your own local situation first: **what exactly is going on here and what could be the best approach** If that approach has proven itself elsewhere, then that is obviously an advantage.

5.2.2 Sources and Examples

When looking for appropriate measures, it certainly does not hurt to first talk to experts who have experience in dealing with High Impact Crime and to also read the examples that are included in this Book of Basics. In addition, there are various national and international databases available as well, starting with our very own ProHIC Knowledge Pearls.

The ProHIC Knowledge Pearls from the Dutch Ministry of Justice and Security

You can first search through the Knowledge Pearls by Jaap de Waard from the Dutch Ministry of Justice and Security. These Knowledge Pearls can be found on the website www. ProHIC.nl and the site's search function makes it easy to scroll through this treasure chest of information. The database chiefly includes synthesis studies or systematic reviews, but also other studies such as government publications or critical commentary on policy and practice. A Knowledge Pearl usually includes a summarised view of knowledge about effective preventive and punitive interventions and measures. The aim is to provide a systematic overview of proven (in)effective measures and interventions. This allows policies to be pursued that are based on reliable facts, thorough analyses and appealing concepts and insights from science and practice. According to Jaap de Waard, this still does not happen enough:

66 *The extent to which available scientific knowledge is used in the preparation of policies can be significantly improved. Underutilisation can be attributed to several reasons. The prevailing culture is one of short-term pragmatism when it*

comes to dealing with political incidents. There is tension between 'policy-based evidence' and 'evidence-based policy' approaches (policy directorates such as that from the 'political secretariats' versus 'evidence-based policy recommendations). In preparing policies, there is a limited collective memory about 'what worked and what did not work' in previous years. **"**

Jaap de Waard
(Kennisparel 200)

Other domestic knowledge databases

(Effective) interventions databases

On a local level this will almost always involve specific tailor-made measures. It is good to know, however, that there are nationally diverse knowledge domains that have extensive databases and careful procedures, such as the recognition procedure for effective youth interventions (**Annex 12**). The databases for effective youth interventions and judicial interventions are especially relevant when it comes to tackling HIC.

The Centre for Crime Prevention and Security (CCV)

The HIC Prevention Guide contains measures that are implemented by municipalities, the police and the Netherlands Public Prosecution Service (Public Prosecutor, OM). The user can first make a selection in the database based on a HIC theme: residential burglaries, armed robberies, street robberies, and violence. The advantage of this site is that it mostly concerns Dutch examples from people that you can easily call/email to ask questions. The disadvantage is that it is a bit like finding a needle in a haystack and there is little to no information available from evaluations as to whether or not an approach works.

For more information, see: https://hetccv.nl/onderwerpen/high-impact-crimes/hic-preventiewijzer/ and also
https://hetccv.nl/onderwerpen/aanpak-overvallen/

International knowledge databases

Popcenter

One international database on measures and approaches that can demonstrably work well is Popcenter, the centre for problem-oriented policing, POP https://popcenter.asu.edu/content/about-us. This site includes about 100 POP guides, Practical documents that discuss specific crime problems and provide ideas on how to tackle them. All guides can be found on: https://popcenter.asu.edu/pop-guides. For HIC specifically, the following guides are the most relevant:[16]

• 'assaults' (number 1, street robberies);
• Armed robbery (numbers 48, 49, 73 and 34);
• Street robberies (number 59);
• burglary (number 18);
• home invasion (number 76).

Be aware that these guides almost always concern material from the United States, Australia or the United Kingdom, and they are not always up to date (> 10 years old). Another possible objection is that the guides pay a lot of attention to the substantive approach and the effect of that approach ('does it work?'), but that the implementation process and preconditions (budget, deployment of people) are often barely discussed. All this information must therefore always be 'translated' to the here and now, and to the specific local context and feasibility. A Dutch translation of the POP approach is also available.[17]

EUPCN and EFUS

In Brussels, a lot of knowledge can be acquired from the European Crime Prevention Network (EUCPN www.eucpn.org). This is an official European (EU) network connecting

---

[16] In addition to these crime-oriented manuals (guides), there are also various manuals for analysis tools. For example, aimed at repeat offenders and repeat victimisation: https://popcenter.asu.edu/content/analyzing-and-responding-repeat-offending en https://popcenter.asu.edu/content/analyzing-repeat-victimization. See under 'tool guides'.

[17] https://www.inholland.nl/onderzoek/publicaties/probleemgericht-werken-en-de-rol-van-criminaliteitsanalyse-in-60-kleine-stappen

local, national and European levels and promoting crime prevention knowledge and practices in all EU Member States since its foundation in 2001.[18] In 2021, an extensive publication was published with the results of the 'EU project Domestic Burglary' https://eucpn.org/document/eu-project-domestic-burglary.

The European Forum for Urban Security (EFUS) www.efus.eu/en also has a vast database of knowledge.

Domestic burglary brochure cover

5.3 Organising measures

A useful instrument for organising the various approaches and measures is a division into three columns: **perpetrator**, **victim** and **situation**.

- What can be done about the problem in a perpetrator-focused way?
- What can victims do, or what can be done on behalf of victims?
- What measures can be taken in the direct environment to make crime less attractive?

This will enable people to come up with initial ideas on approaches/measures. What is often immediately apparent, is that only some columns will have a list of potential solutions, whereas other columns will remain almost completely empty. All this while the key to fighting crime lies in a truly integrated approach. But if certain columns are left empty, at least you know what aspects of your approach need to be addressed further. Columns that remain (relatively) empty obviously require more attention!

Further fine-tuning is sometimes undertaken by distinguishing between the different types of prevention (primary, secondary and tertiary). See **Annex 19**.

Example of a diagram: Armed robberies: measures aimed at **perpetrators, victims** and **situations**

Measures	
Perpetrators	• Repression: identification and prosecution of perpetrators (by the police and Public Prosecutor, permanent public prosecutor for armed robberies and (ram-raids/explosives used in e.g. safe-cracking etc)
	• Data collection by the police
	• Perpetrator (group) analysis by the police
	• Confiscation of criminally acquired assets, financial investigations also for the purpose of seizure of victims' stolen property
	• Improving quality and placement of (mobile) camera surveillance
	• Distribution of digital doorbells throughout the entire neighbourhood
	• Installing (more) cameras in the neighbourhood, see *Camera in Beeld* www.politie.nl/onderwerpen/camera-in-beeld.html
	• Theft prevention kits
	• Perpetrator-oriented communication; physical space and via (social) media
	• Structural, integrated preventive approach to 'problematic young people' (potential offenders)
Victims	• Victim support for companies, staff and customers

Victims

- A GPS tracking system (such as Track and Trace) for valuable products

- Claim for damages following a robbery

- Contact person for armed robbery crimes located at the police and branch organisation for information and services

- Location and/or industry-oriented communication about armed robberies

  > Armed robbery training especially for branch managers, so that they can transfer their knowledge to their staff

- Preventing victimisation in companies

  > Organisation

    - Establishing procedures and instructions
    - Agree that any deviations from normal day-to-day practice should be reported
    - Staff training
    - Presence of two or more staff members
    - Presence of a security employee

  > Architectural measures/circumstances

    - Security of entrances
    - Clear company layout
    - Controllable entrances and exits
    - Good visibility from the outside
    - Another operating company in the close vicinity
    - Secure cash register/cash storage area
    - No keys that can be easily copied without knowing the code
    - Use a shop bell, so you know when someone enters a shop
    - Opt for locks with the SKG logo
    - Place poles in front of the shop to prevent ram raids
    - Secure the safe onto the floor

  > Technical provisions

    - Protection and shielding of cash and securities
    - Limit the amount of directly available cash (set a limit)

Victims	<ul><li>Use a time-delayed safe for removing surplus cash</li><li>Preferably use a safe with a deposit slot at the cash register</li><li>Always remove any surplus money away from the view of customers</li><li>Immediately put the name of your company on checks, making them unusable for thieves</li><li>Put the daily revenue in a safe that uses a time delay</li><li>Promote more debit card usage when working in vulnerable sectors</li><li>Conditional opening of safes; use safe detectors</li><li>Panic and burglar alarms (including panic button) Neighbourhood Help System Camera installation + connection to Live View, see www.politie.nl/informatie/zo-werkt-live-view.html</li><li>(Professional) money transport</li></ul>
Situation	<ul><li>Design the (shopping) area in such a way that high-risk companies are located at locations where there is a lot of traffic and where there are no open escape routes</li><li>Pay special attention to theft risks in urban renewal plans and General Municipal By-laws</li><li>Surveillance (police, security services) at high-risk times (days, months)</li></ul>

Go to/Fill in for 'your problem'

For the problem you are dealing with in your municipality together with the project group, you can now fill in the empty matrix below in a similar way as above.

Measures
Perpetrators
Victims
Situation

5.4 Determining prerequisites

Prerequisites include matters such as money, commitment of time, people and knowledge. For each measure, questions such as:

- the size of the budget required,

- the source(s) of financing,

- how many and which people need to be mobilised (staff, planning and hours),

- are new staff required,

- does everyone have the knowledge and motivation to do the job,

- is any further training required,

- are any additional facilities, buildings or premises needed? If yes, which ones?

These kinds of practical and essential questions must always be answered before starting the procedures. This can easily be done by linking the set of measures with a number of questions/columns (see **5.3.**).

Go to/Fill in for 'your problem'

	Measures	Expenditure	Budget	Time investment	Start/finish	Who	Other	Other
Perpetrators								
Victims								
Situation								

5.5 Proposal for an evaluation

An evaluation is something that you do after you have implemented measures, right? Not really! In fact, this is the most commonly made mistake. Once the measures have been implemented, it then turns out that the situation was not defined properly beforehand, that figures/data are no longer available, that it was not properly documented what exactly was done by whom. A sound evaluation calls for proper consideration beforehand (!), i.e., now. A plan should also be made for it, with the first question being "Are we actually going to evaluate this (project, approach, scheme)?' See chapter 6 for more details, but before starting the approach, first answer all the pressing questions concerning the evaluation (effect and/or process evaluation) and also fill in, for example, **Annex 20** in order to get a concrete idea of the kinds of questions you need to or want to answer.

5.6 Will this work?

If we look at the whole package of measures that is now in the pipeline, the question has to be asked: will this work? Under the motto 'better to stop half way than to fail completely', the following checks on the action plan are important:

1 Is there a proper **focus**? The approach should focus on the causes of HIC, and whether they are the fault of the perpetrator(s), victim(s) or are due to the situation (location, place, neighbourhood, time).

2 Is there a **balanced package of measures**? There is often a smart combination of various measures - both preventive and punitive - that are implemented from various sides (and therefore properly coordinated by the different actors).

Can the parties involved actually implement the measures? Do they have the time, money and permission to do this? See 5.4 Preconditions and also take the evaluation into account (if indeed an evaluation is needed/obligatory: what does an evaluation take/cost? see 5.5. and chapter 6).

3 Does the whole package of planned measures have the **desired effect** and are there no potential negative side effects? Special care must be taken to ensure that the adopted measures do not lead to stigmatisation, for one thing. If you give specific neighbourhoods or groups a lot of attention, you also set those neighbourhoods and groups apart.

4 Has the **evaluation** process been properly arranged in **advance**?

5 Last but not least: is the approach to the problem being managed properly? Without **proper management** from the triangle and project group, the measures are doomed to fail. Who is the first point of contact and person in charge within the triangle and project group?

Also see the B3W matrix about a more effective approach to residential burglaries www.politieacademie.nl/kennisenonderzoek/kennis/mediatheek/pdf/89054.pdf *(Versteegh & Hesseling, 2013)*.

5.7 Result: A joint Action Plan

With all the work that has been outlined above, a joint Action Plan (AP) can now be easily drawn up. This Action Plan for the local triangle is usually set up by the police team chief and the municipal head of Public Order and Security.[19] It contains a brief overview of the analysis of the previously prioritised HIC problem, the goals to be achieved, measures to be implemented and an initial plan for a possible evaluation of the process and effect.

At this time, it is recommended to re-examine the composition of the project group (**are all the organisations involved on board with the plan?**) and to determine how often reporting back to the triangle should take place. These aspects should be formalised and recorded in writing. The project group is now responsible for the implementation of the project: the measures and the evaluation.

Example of a possible Action Plan table of contents:

Introduction

1. Previously set priorities concerning HIC (originating from the regional or local policy plan and/or safety plan).

2. HIC definitions.

---

[19] These can involve the analyst, operational specialists and municipal researcher.

3. Results of the problem analysis or problem analyses with regard to location, time, perpetrator(s) and victim. Who, what, where, when, why, with what, and in what way?

4. Suggested approach:

- Goals: what concrete results do we want to achieve with regard to each W (see 3)? And: are we going to evaluate the degree to which the goals are (being) achieved before/ during or after? If so, how?

- Measures: who will do what and when? What will each measure cost (in terms of both effort/time and money) and who will pay for it?

- Do we record the implementation process for the purpose of a process evaluation? If so, how? What does the overall intent and the plan for evaluation (effect/process) look like?

- How is the communication organised, both internally and externally?

- How much will it cost in terms of time (and whose time exactly)?

- Lead time.

- Risk section.

5. Information about the role and staffing of the project group.

An example from practice. https://rsiv.nl/kennisbank/highimpactcrimes/woninginbraken/.

5.8 The triangle approves the Action Plan

Now that there is a plan of action on the table, the triangle must make a final decision. In many cases, some adjustments will have to be made before the triangle approves it.

5.9 Summary

____

Formulate specific goals using the SMART method

• Specific • Measurable • Attainable • Realistic • Timely

____

Determine the measures by describing why and how they contribute to achieving the goal. There are plenty of sources for proven, effective measures, for example:

• ProHIC Knowledge Pearls • Databases • CCV • POPcenter • EUPCN and EFUS

____

One can organise measures by placing them in a diagram based on the crime triangle: perpetrator, victim and situation.

____

Check your Action Plan:

1. Is there a focus?

2. Is there a balanced set of measures? Can the parties involved actually implement the measures? Do they have the time, money and permission to do so?

3. Do the set of measures have the desired effect and are there no potential negative side effects?

4. Has the evaluation process been properly organised in advance?

5. Is the approach being managed effectively? Who is the first point of contact and person in charge within the triangle?

Result: An Action Plan for the local triangle by the police team chief and the municipal head of Public Order and Security, with a brief overview of the analysis of the previously prioritised HIC problem, the goals to be achieved, measures to be implemented and an initial plan for an eventual evaluation of the process and impact.

Tackling Hot Shots

A Top approach for hot shots

A relatively small number of offenders commit a disproportionate amount of crime. These frequent repeat offenders, 'revolving door' criminals or systematic offenders are also referred to by the term 'hot shots'. One typical approach, which focuses on the perpetrators of HIC, consists of getting a general idea of these perpetrators' behaviour and applying a special approach to them.

Dordrecht 1990 Top Approach

In the 1990s, the city of Dordrecht created a so-called TOP list of Systematic Offenders. These offenders entered a special project known as the IBA (Intensieve Begeleidings Aanpak, Intensive Supervision Approach). Supervision was provided by the social services (work/unemployment benefit service), housing company/housing corporation (housing), probation service, police, the Public Prosecutor, judges and the municipality (overall supervision in the context of neighbourhood management). This multi-angled approach proved to be demonstrably effective at the time *(Bruinink & Lagendijk, 1994)*. One strong point was that the approach was part of a much broader neighbourhood-oriented approach to neighbourhood management and crime prevention *(Bruinink et al., 1994)*; an approach that resulted from the

Dutch government's memorandum on Criminal Justice through Policy. The
Dordrecht approach was subsequently exported to the UK *(Chenery & Pease,
2000)* and proved to be effective there as well.[20]

Amsterdam 2010 Top 600

A delegation from the Amsterdam municipality picked up on what they saw
as the new spectacular overseas approach in England, as there was a problem
in Amsterdam with a lot of HIC at the time, including a lot of violent armed
robberies and aggravated assault. In 2010, it was decided to establish an
approach aimed at tackling residential burglaries, armed robberies, street
robberies, aggravated assault, public violence and murder/manslaughter:
20 years later in Amsterdam, the Dordrecht TOP approach became the
Top 600 approach.

Analysis

The approach is aimed at 600 criminal repeat offenders who are responsible for
more than 15,000 HIC cases (according to the broad definition as mentioned
above). Further analyses have also demonstrated that the problems of these
criminals are often multi-faceted. For example, difficulties surrounding 'income,
debt, housing and care, and an environment with many risk factors (such as friends
who are 'known' to the police) often play a role *(Van Grinsven & Verwest, 2017)*.

Measures

The aim of the Top 600 approach is to reduce HIC recidivism, improve the future
prospects of Top 600 people and reduce the influx of new offenders. Based on
the analysis of the problem in the municipality of Amsterdam, it was decided to
tackle crime with three measures *(Verwest, 2016)*:

1. **Directly (lik-op-stuk): taking swift, consistent and strict action**
   This means an acceleration in the criminal justice chain - from Public
   Prosecutor to court to prison. For example, the judiciary set up a 'fast lane'
   for appeal cases especially for the Top 600, so that they can be heard
   within three months.

2. **Care: mandatory screening and care as a permanent element in
   addition to the sentence**
   Screening provides insight into the psychological state and intellectual
   capacity of the offender. In addition, it is about gaining insight into
   housing needs, daytime activities, lifestyle and the need for learning/work

---

[20] See Kennisparel 12*. Also: Braga et al.,2019 and for the UK: Dawson & Cuppleditch, 2007.

* More information about sources, see the digital version at www.prohic.nl

trajectories. This also means that the Top 600 individual can be placed in an appropriate care programme.

3. **Restriction of inflow: a family-oriented approach in the interest of brothers and sisters**
Through intervention in the family, by screening brothers and sisters and by ensuring that they go to school and obtain a basic qualification, special attention is paid to a Top 600 individual's family and their direct living environment.

Integrated work method

A large number of people on the Top 600 list already had prior contact with various (aid) organisations, from probation to debt counselling, from the Public Prosecutor to youth care centres. However, none of these organisations were responsible for overseeing the individual's situation as a whole. They had a piece of the puzzle, as it were, but none of them had the task of putting the puzzle together. This changed with the Top 600 approach. Under the direction of the Municipality of Amsterdam, more than 40 different partner organisations are participating in the Top 600 approach. These are organisations from domains such as security, care and social services.

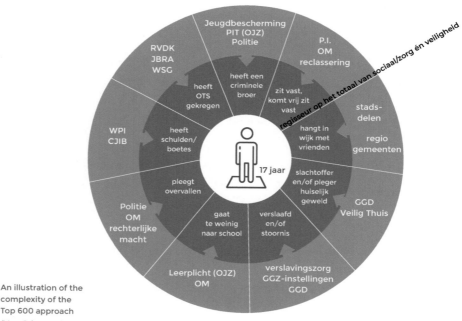

An illustration of the complexity of the Top 600 approach
(Van Grinsven & Verwest, 2017)

Manager

A individual manager is appointed for each individual on the Top 600 list. The manager works as a link between the various organisations that the individual on the list is involved in. For example, the director, together with these organisations and the Top 600 individual, may draw up an action plan aimed at the specific situation of the individual in question.

Results

At the start of the Top 600 approach, there were 1,391 individuals on the list. At the end of 2018, the list comprised 469 people. In other words, 922 people no longer met the requirements for inclusion on the list and were removed from it. In 2018, it became clear that from the moment the Top 600 approach was implemented, recidivism decreased by 41%. When it came to HIC, this was even 50% *(Van Grinsven & Verwest, 2017)*. For those who left the list, the recidivism rate was even less in terms of HIC, 82% lower. In addition to reducing the risk of recidivism, progress has also been made in other areas, such as improving self-reliance, care, work, income and a successful return to society after detention. The Top 600 approach is seen as a very successful approach - often referencing these results. Critical questions have nevertheless been raised about this. For example, crime is declining throughout the Netherlands (including HIC), but this reduction is actually less in Amsterdam than in the three other largest municipalities. At the same time, age may also play a role in the decline in recidivism among people on the Top 600 list. The peak age of delinquency is on average 18 years old, after which it drops by 5 percent per year *(Berghuis, 2018)*. The average age of individuals on the list has slowly risen over the years, which partly explains the decline in recidivism *(Beijersbergen et al., 2018)*.

It therefore cannot be claimed with complete certainty that the Top 600 approach in Amsterdam is effective. Other (international) research (including Braga et al. 2019) shows that comparable approaches with a focus on repeat offenders can certainly be effective.

Other cities

Over the years, the Amsterdam Top 600 approach has become more widely adopted throughout the Netherlands. Today, it is being implemented in several municipalities (including Utrecht and Gouda, for example). It is a good example of a focused approach that puts the (systematic) offender or repeat offender at the centre, thereby keeping an eye on their complete living environment (housing, work, family, health/addiction, education, friends). An approach that focuses on the care and attention for the perpetrator, but one that is backed up by concrete sanctions. Prevention with a bite. It is quite remarkable that an innovative idea conceived in 1990 in Dordrecht is subsequently forgotten in the Netherlands to only reappear 20 years later - via another country. With this Top 600 approach, the question arises whether attention cannot be paid to repeat offenders at an even earlier stage? For example, can problematic young people be prevented from progressing (via HIC) to serious organised crime? This is a particularly important question if we look at the many murders, assassinations and complicated/expensive lawsuits that are currently taking place in the Netherlands.

From 'upcoming talent' to the hardcore group

Research into the characteristics and developments of problematic youth groups *(Ferwerda et al., 2017)* found that 'youth groups that are guilty of disruptive behaviour are predominantly neighbourhood-based. Groups that cause trouble (nuisance) tend to operate across neighbourhoods, while criminal youth groups have the largest operating radius and also operate regionally and nationally' *(Ferwerda & Van Wijk, 2010)*. As the operating radius increases, the groups withdraw from the public domain, are less guilty of causing visible nuisance and focus more on committing crimes. In this stage of development, criminal youth groups slowly but surely disappear from the streets and develop into supra-local criminal networks. The police, the justice department and other security partners therefore lose sight of these groups, because police supervision is mainly organised in a neighbourhood-oriented manner. It is then regularly incorrectly suggested that 'the problem has been solved', after which the focus moves on to a different youth group *(Beke et al., 2013)*.

Research into 'recruitment' and 'promotion' in an increasingly complex criminal 'career' is still very much in its infancy. What is certain, however, is that organised crime is a different type of crime compared to 'common adolescent neighbourhood nuisance/petty crime'. In organised crime, for example, social relationships of trust play a much more important role *(Kleemans & Van Koppen, 2014)*. Recruitment for organised crime and terrorism appears to follow very similar patterns *(Weisburd et al., 2020)*.[21]

---

[21] In any case, there is a significant relationship between terrorists and 'ordinary criminals' with regard to behaviour, motivation, demographic characteristics and protective and risk factors. Also see Kennisparel 90* en Wolfowicz et al., 2019.

This type of research carries an important warning: do not just assess the situation on a local level.

66 *Safety policy is chiefly oriented and organised locally. As a result, there is relatively little insight into so-called supra-local crime and its possible relationship with local crime.* 99

(Ferwerda et al., 2017)

Dutch research *(Ferwerda et al., 2013)* **shows that**

66 *supra-local network formation could form a direct threat to local safety levels and that there is a risk of crime spreading on a local level. Successful hardcore crime groups often serve as a shining example that crime pays and, in this sense, are a negative role model for the rising stars in particular. In fact, sometimes 'hardcore' crime groups pick out criminal talent from local networks (recruitment). By doing that, this group feeds local crime in several ways. They can have an almost invisible effect on a neighbourhood. The fact that there are families that facilitate crime and also benefit from it is illustrative of this. (...). First of all, there is a task at the local (municipal) level when it comes to dealing with young recruits who, unlike the average young troublemaker, are already part of a criminal network. When setting up an approach for tackling crime, it is important for municipalities but also other security partners (including the Regional Information and Expertise Centre / RIEC), to know who the facilitators are and which criminal families are active in the municipality. Furthermore, the police (investigators) and the justice department could focus on the small number of criminal leaders in networks. Identifying and dealing with these leaders, in combination with an approach for other groups, will have a disruptive effect on the entire network.* 99

See Kennisparel 79[*]

6. Evaluation

- The evaluation plan, as prepared in advance (see Action Plan), has been implemented. What are the results?

- List these results and report on them (if required). At a minimum, record and communicate the results for yourself and for those involved.

- What can be learned from this evaluation as far as the process is concerned (what went well/not as well) and the effect (output, outcome and impact)? What worked, what did not and are there any particularly encouraging signs?

It cannot be repeated enough: it is crucial that there is an evaluation plan in place before the start of the Action Plan is implemented. The first question should be: do we actually want (or should we) evaluate what we are going to do? If the particular approach has been applied before and if an evaluation is not requested (for example, by subsidy providers, Netherlands Court of Audit/the municipal council or senior managers[22]), why would you even carry out an evaluation? Politicians and police chiefs are by no means always a fan of evaluations. For example, there is a risk that the goals will not be (completely) achieved, things may already have gone wrong while implementing the measures and the process may have cost a lot more time and been a lot more expensive than expected. In addition, evaluation costs time and often money. Most of all, it is not an easy task.[23]

However, if you want to learn something, then an evaluation cannot be avoided. At the bare minimum, it should be possible to sit down with all stakeholders halfway through or at the end of a project to discuss what went well and what could be improved. The most important results from this meeting can then be recorded on a piece of A4 paper (**Annex 20**). However, sometimes more is required. People who have to account for their actions often cannot avoid a more formal evaluation. In many cases, however, a simple process evaluation is sufficient.

If the decision is made that an evaluation will be carried out, this means the following: matters must be properly recorded and documented before and during the process, time and money must be made available for an evaluation and sometimes external parties even need to be engaged.[24] Sometimes it can also be beneficial to work with (standardised) self-evaluation instruments *(Versteegh et al., 2015; Van Dijk et al., 2015).*

---

[22] Tip: if there are 'higher powers' who are requesting or even insisting on an evaluation, ask beforehand what this person/party (for whom it is being created for) are expecting from this. For example, should it be an impact evaluation and/or a process evaluation? Often, it is 'just' a matter of asking for a justification (for accounting purposes). Making things transparent in advance provides clarity and helps to avoid too much work!

[23] As a rule of thumb, it is assumed that a proper evaluation of new and important policies requires a mark-up of 10-15% on the project/policy implementation costs where hours/costs are concerned.

[24] Tip: only outsource an evaluation if the approach is completely new, the stakes are high, or a lot of effort/money is involved.

There are many things to consider during an evaluation:

→ **Effect (output, outcome and impact)**

- **Output**: the achievements of these activities.

- **Outcome**: the direct effects of these achievements.

- **Impact**: the changes ultimately achieved in society.

During an evaluation, it is common practice to distinguish between 'impact evaluation' (which looks at output, but mainly outcomes and impact) and 'process evaluation' (which focuses on input and activities).[25]

→ **Process (input and throughput)**

- Input: people and resources that are mobilised.

- Measures/activities: the interventions and instruments that are implemented with these resources (sometime referred to as throughput).

---

[25] For more information, also see: www.rijksbegroting.nl/beleidsevaluaties/evaluaties-en-beleidsdoorlichtingen/handreiking-beleidsdoorlichtingen/het-meten-van-doeltreffendheid. A lot of information about evaluations is available internationally too. For example, see steps 46 and 47 of 60 steps: https://popcenter.asu.edu/sites/default/files/library/reading/PDFs/60steps_dutch.pdf or a manual of the EUCPN: https://eucpn.org/sites/default/files/document/files/20140310_toolboxmanual_translationnl_0.pdf.

6.1 Impact evaluation

The impact evaluation examines whether, and to what extent, the established goals (and any sub-goals) have been achieved and what their impact is. Questions for impact evaluation:

- Has the main goal been achieved? To what extent?

- Have the various sub-goals been achieved? To what extent? Which have/haven't?

- Has achieving the sub-goals lead to achieving the main goal?

- Sometimes this is followed by a question related to a broader (social) impact: the changes ultimately achieved in society.

The first two questions are intended purely as an assessment; certain criteria (target numbers) have been set and it is checked whether these criteria have been met. The third and fourth questions are of an explanatory nature; you endeavour to demonstrate that the realisation of the sub-goals has led to the realisation of the main goal and that this has subsequently also had a broader social impact. In other words: the realisation of measures X, for example installing burglary-proof hinges and locks in all homes in neighbourhood A, has led to a demonstrable reduction in problem Y by Z% (for example, 40% less burglaries in neighbourhood A).

The subsequent impact questions are even broader: has neighbourhood A now become 'safer' than before? Is neighbourhood A doing better than neighbourhoods B and C? Do people feel safer and/or has the image of the neighbourhood improved?

From the third question onwards, things get a bit trickier. There are two reasons for this: *the scatter gun problem and the crime displacement problem.*

The scatter gun problem

A lot of measures are taken in the hope that together, they will achieve the desired outcome. For example: 'The number of burglaries in this municipality will decline from 135 in 2019 to 50 in 2020'. So, burglary prevention (Police Label Safe and Secure Housing) is being carried out, but the youth groups are also being tackled and there is an approach to multi-problem families (MPF) in the municipality. If the main goal has actually been achieved (we are down from 135 burglaries to 50 one year later), then what are the reasons for that? The youth workers know this, of course, but so do the people from the MPF initiative, and it is also perfectly clear to the Police Inspectorate.

Moreover, the social impact hasn't even been discussed at this stage: do residents in the neighbourhood feel safer? Is the feeling of a lack of safety declining, and is trust in others/police increasing (as a result)? Is the neighbourhood viewed differently now? By local residents and/or outsiders?

The crime displacement problem

When we consider a phenomenon such as 'crime displacement effects', things can become even more complicated. For example, various measures aimed at neighbourhood A may reduce residential burglaries in that neighbourhood. A great outcome of course, but what if it turns out that the burglaries in the adjacent neighbourhoods B and C suddenly increase? The impact, the eventual 'social change', can then even be a net negative. Things become even more complex if the effects in neighbourhood B and C - where no measures have been taken - are also positive. This is quite a common phenomenon and is referred to as *the diffusion of benefits*.

Crime displacement comes in many shapes and sizes: in terms of time (from day to night, from summer to winter), in terms of purpose (a secure home A is skipped and the burglar chooses an unsecured home B or a school/neighbourhood building), in terms of location/area (from area X to area Y), in terms of tactics/ modus operandi (the robber uses a gun instead of a knife) and finally in terms of type of crime (home burglaries are becoming increasingly difficult so the burglar specialises in armed robberies and street robberies instead). Incidentally, the effects of crime displacement are generally not as bad as they seem, and there are at least as many positive side effects. For more information, see the POP tools guide from the international crime displacement expert Rob Guerette (2009). Also see: Hesseling, 1994, 'Stoppen of verplaatsen?' And for a convenient overview, see Knowledge Pearl 9*.

In order to keep a clear view of the consequences in all of this, an identical control area is actually needed, to check out what the developments are there. For example, think about studies into the efficacy of medicines and vaccine trials that are carried out in 'double-blind' tests. Everyone gets a pill, but one pill has an active substance and the other one doesn't. Who gets which pill is determined strictly by chance (randomisation). Unfortunately, such a stringent approach is not really possible for neighbourhoods and districts.

In order to keep things workable, a key requirement of an impact evaluation is to have goals that:

• are defined in terms of the desired (end) result;

• are defined in measurable terms.

This may seem easy, but it is often not possible due to carelessness and haste ('let's get started as quickly as possible'), or due to more or less hidden differences in the goals that participating parties have.

Moreover, whoever wants to check whether the realisation of the (sub) goals has directly resulted in achieving the overarching main goal, will have to consider the following:

• there must be a goal-resources chain or policy theory in place, in which the causal relationships between the main goal, sub-goals and measures are clearly defined.

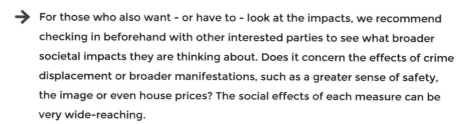

→ For those who also want - or have to - look at the impacts, we recommend checking in beforehand with other interested parties to see what broader societal impacts they are thinking about. Does it concern the effects of crime displacement or broader manifestations, such as a greater sense of safety, the image or even house prices? The social effects of each measure can be very wide-reaching.

* More information about sources, see the digital version at www.prohic.nl

6.2 Process evaluation

The process evaluation looks at how the policy/project proceeded in practice: what was done and how did it go? The input of time, money, people, knowledge and the implemented measures and activities. A process evaluation can be handled in either a narrow or a broader way. A narrow process evaluation limits itself to the execution of the project. In addition to the execution of the policy/project, a broad process evaluation also examines the preparation of the policy/project, including all project planning steps, and examines the environment of the project.

Process evaluation can be even more important in those cases where the impact is very difficult to determine or measure (e.g., in the case of subversion, drug trafficking, human trafficking, cybercrime). In this case, the question of whether what is required (evidence-based) has actually been implemented becomes increasingly more important. If this is the case, then perhaps the effect may be considered plausible, so we then move on to a more qualitative mode of management and accountability.

Both in national and international research, the importance of a thorough process evaluation - and an adequate recording thereof - is still underestimated. An approach from the United States may be presented as effective in an 'evidence-based' sense, but how useful is this information in a Dutch setting, when the budget and commitment in the US is many times greater? Which is why, in addition to the question of '**what was achieved?**', the question of '**what was done and how was it done?**' is also just as important.

Potential(!) questions for a process evaluation can be found in **Annex 21**. Quite a few - very good - questions can be considered (> 100). Therefore, mainly use the list from the appendix to select which questions really need to be asked (and consequently which ones can be dropped). Of course, any fool could ask a lot more, but then ...

6.3 Summary

However, if you want to learn something, then an evaluation cannot be avoided. At a minimum, you can sit down with all those invelved at the halfway point or at the end of a project to discuss what went well and what could be improved.

If more is required, you could consider an impact and/or process evaluation too.

In an impact evaluation, it is important that the goals in the Action Plan are formulated according to the SMART method so th<t they are easy to evaluate. you take a look at:

• Output • Outcome • Impact

If you wish to check wheter the realisation of the (sub)goals has directly resulted in achieving the overarching main goal, you will have to consider the following:

• Is a goal-resources chain or policy theory in place, in which the casual relationships between the main goal, sub-goals and measures are clearly defined.

A process evaluation deals with the people involved, the instruments on hand and the resources. You consider the following:

• Input • Throughput

Tackling Residential Burglaries in Gouda

Burglaries have long been a persistent problem in Gouda. In 2016, for example, Gouda had the highest burglary risk of all municipalities in the Netherlands, with 20 burglaries per 1,000 households. This is twice as high as the average for the entire Hague police unit. This was one of the reasons for the police unit to draw up a memorandum ('Towards a sustained reduction of residential burglaries', adopted during the Regional Management Meeting of The Hague police unit on 29 June 2017) with the ambition to reduce the burglary risk in Gouda and a number of other municipalities down to 8 burglaries per 1,000 households.

The figures also showed that a significant concentration of residential burglaries occurred in the Goverwelle neighbourhood. In order to tackle this problem, from 2017 onwards, the new team leadership of the Gouda Local Policing Unit of the police has been working together with the municipality, housing associations and residents to reduce the number of residential burglaries. To this end, a problem-oriented approach according to the 'Best of three worlds (B3W)' has been implemented.

The table below provides an overview of the measures that have been initiated since 2017.

Maatregelen probleemgerichte aanpak
Gouda Goverwelle

Dadergerichte maatregelen	Slachtoffergerichte maatregelen/ burgerparticipatie	Omgevingsgerichte maatregelen
Top 60 aanpak	Matrixborden	Subsidieregelingen voor inbraakwerende maatregelen en poortverlichting (deze regelingen zijn in heel Gouda van kracht)
Aanpak criminele families	Tent in de wijk	
Aanpak jeugdoverlast	Besmettings-/informatie-borden	
Kort cyclische aanpak opspring	Flyeren over inbraakpreventie	Omgevingsgerichte maatregelen
Voorkomen nieuwe aanwas	Video met stroomschema voor meldingen door huisartsen en andere zorgpartners	
	Opbouwwerkster	
	Buurtpreventieteam	
	Buurtbooth	
	Bewonersbijeenkomsten en -activiteiten	
	Inzet (sociale) media	
	Buurtinitiatiefgroep 't Govertje	
	Buurtvaders	

An innovative measure is the approach to criminal families. The approach is described as a *systems approach*, which looks at the role of family members who maintain the 'criminal family system'. The following partners are involved: police (team chief, individual-centred team, neighbourhood police officer), municipality (safety/crisis manager, youth coordinator, process director Top 600, Integrated Safety Policy consultant), RIEC (Regional Information and Expertise Centre), Safety House, Public Prosecutor, housing corporations and various other (security) organisations. For the investigation and prosecution of burglaries, particularly of homes, the police have taken organisational measures with specific attention given to Goverwelle, in order to be able to work more efficiently and effectively. The method is described as a short-cycle approach, which is 'much more action-oriented'. The Local Policing Unit of the police has been given access to the flex team of the entire Alphen aan de Rijn district, of which the Gouda Local Policing Unit is a part of. This flex team has been given a mandate to set up larger investigations without the need to scale up further.

Reduction in residential burglaries

The implemented measures have led to a significant reduction in the number of burglaries. Although the sharpest reduction has been seen in Goverwelle, the rest of Gouda has also benefited from the measures.

Less trouble is caused on the streets by young people

Both professionals and residents indicated that from 2016 onwards they expected less trouble on the streets. The incarceration of some of the young people who caused a lot of the problems is also cited as an important factor here.

More sharing of information between residents and police

The community police officer in Goverwelle has had intensive contact with residents, including members of the criminal families and their immediate social circles. This has resulted in an improved information exchange with a group of residents that are difficult to reach. Trust between these residents and the police has increased, according to those involved. Another positive aspect of this is that members of criminal families no longer feel untouchable and that interaction with members and social circles of the criminal families has improved. According to the police, a more respectful outreach is taking place and the police are generally receiving more information from these residents.

This may have also contributed to the increase in the clearance rate that began in 2018. After all, some of the burglaries are solved thanks to reports from residents.

Joint activities of residents

Low levels of social control and growing polarisation were identified at the start of the approach as key areas of concern. Whether social control in the neighbourhood has increased and/or polarisation has diminished is difficult to determine. However, according to those involved, positive developments have been initiated in this area as well.

Collaboration between police and municipality

Lastly, according to those involved, cooperation between the municipality, police and other partners has improved. This cooperation has contributed significantly to the results, so those involved say.

Appendices

Annex 1

Safety Monitor (VM, VeiligheidsMonitor)

We have noticed that a lot of crime, roughly two-thirds,[26] is not or rarely reported to the police, and the police do not have a clear sense of what is going on. Fortunately, a lot of reports are made to the police about burglaries, armed robberies and street robberies (HIC), so that is not so much of a problem in this regard. But anyone who wants to look more broadly than just at these three HIC problems would do well to look not only at police information, but definitely also at the information on victims in the Security Monitor (VM) from Statistics Netherlands).

The VM is an extensive biannual survey in which researchers from Statistics Netherlands ask Dutch people (over 100,000 respondents) about victimisation, not feeling safe, quality of life, neighbourhood trouble spots (nuisance levels), the police and community-based prevention. This information is neatly arranged in a huge interactive database https:// veiligheidsmonitor.databank.nl/. It contains everything in the Safety Monitor (VeiligheidsMonitor) from Satistic Netherlands (CBS) for Local Policing Units, districts and teams, but also for provinces and municipalities (> 70,000 residents).[27]

> The Safety Monitor (VM) starts with a pie chart that at a glance shows per area (province, municipality, unit, district) where this region or municipality scores better or worse in terms of the various Local Policing Unit themes on safe/non-safe situations compared to the national average: victimisation, liveability, nuisance in the neighbourhood, perception of safety, police and citizens, and prevention. Based on this information, local and regional policymakers can see which themes deserve more or less attention (prioritisation).

---

[26] The situation is actually much worse, because here we make a comparison between the national research on victims (Safety Monitor) and the police reports in the Netherlands. Companies, institutions, tourists and victimless criminal offences (such as drug abuse) are not reflected in the Safety Monitor.

[27] Please note: the Safety Monitor concerns information about households and individuals. It is a public survey. Information about companies or institutions requires other sources. See: https://www.wodc.nl/binaries/cr2012-hoofdstuk-3_tcm28-73134.pdf (p. 64 and beyond) and https://www.wodc.nl/binaries/ob279-bijlage3_tcm28-71064.pdf. Locally, there is often more or other types of information available. Consult local specialists at the municipality.

You can see the underlying values per theme by clicking on a section in the chart. A dynamic report can be created for each main theme within the Safety Monitor. Furthermore, on this page the user can view a core report (a combination of the six sub-reports) and a summary fact sheet about the region in question (download or print).

The application is opened by clicking 'Databank' in the menu.

Via 'Support', the user gains access to the online manual of Swing Viewer (the software that is used to access the Safety Monitor). In addition, a reading guide has been included in the database to support novice users.

In short: this is an enormous toolkit for tools that can be used in prioritising and analysing the local safety situation. A similar toolkit also exists for police data: https://data. politie.nl.[28]

It is important to realise that the Safety Monitor includes many more crimes that individuals and households have fallen victim to, but the old adage applies here in both cases:

Every advantage has a disadvantage.

For example, the Safety Monitor includes absolutely no information about companies and organisations. A school where there is a burglary will, after reporting, be included in the police database, but not in the Safety Monitor. The same applies for supermarket thefts. Even a tourist or expat who is mugged on the street does not end up registered in the Safety Monitor, whereas there is a possibility that they will end up in the police database. The same is true for so-called 'victimless crimes' (think of drugs etc.). Furthermore, the VM 'measures' in a way that makes use of the words of the average Dutch citizen - it is, after all, a survey - and does not use precise criminal law categories. There are even more tricky differences. In the Safety Monitor, for example, there is no distinction between a residential burglary and an attempt thereto, even though attempts may be a 'preventive success' ('they didn't get into the house!'). In this case, the police database is more precise and, for instance, goes much deeper into the perpetrator's modus operandi.

28 Source: https://veiligheidsmonitor.databank.nl//jive/jivereportcontents.ashx?report=home_informatie (consulted March 2020).

Annex 2

Integrated Security Policy (IVB)

Guidelines and formats under the framework of the municipal Integrated Safety Policy

- Kernbeleid Veiligheid 2021: handreiking voor gemeenten (Core Policy Safety 2021: guideline for municipalities) (pdf)*
- Rapportage veiligheidsanalyse 2021-2024 (Security Analysis Report 2021-2024) (word)*
- Integrated Safety Plan (IVP) (word)*
- Implementation Plan (word)*

Also

- Centre for Crime Prevention and Security: instruments for integrated safety policy**
- Basisboek integrale veiligheid *(Stol et al., 2016)*

Annex 3

Intelligence-led Policing (ILP)

Intelligence-led policing is essentially about the question

'Are we doing the right things and are we doing the right things effectively?'

Within this approach, data, information, knowledge and intelligence (intelligent action) (Politieacademie, 2013, informatiegestuurd politiewerk) are defined.

---

* More information about sources, see the digital version at www.vng.nl

** More information about sources, see the digital version at www.hetccv.nl

66 *Everything we hear and see on the street and everything that is observed by police officers is recorded in our organisation's dedicated systems. This results in the creation of* **data***: raw data that has to be filtered out. As soon as these data have been checked, gaps have been filled in and contradictions have been removed (filtered out) and we can start to interpret this data or place it in a certain context, then we are talking about* **information***. When we then combine this information with other information and existing (scientific) insights and then establish connections between the different types of information, that's what we refer to as* **knowledge***. Intelligence comes after this, namely action-oriented information that may lead to police action.* 99

Incidentally, action that is taken is then evaluated again for its effect, after which the cycle is repeated *(see the arrow in the figure).*

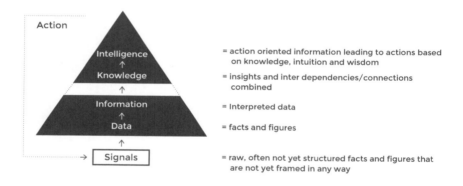

The Intelligence-led policing model (ILP) mainly focuses on the police as analysts and actors. See the terminology used: 'police officers notice', 'recorded in the dedicated systems of our organisation' and 'that may lead to police action'. In essence, the model works according to the following formula: police data in → police action out. Eyes and ears belong to the police and steer their hands and feet. The approach in this Book of Basics is based on a broader interpretation (with the municipality, the Netherlands Public Prosecution Service, citizens/residents and companies/institutions). After all, the responsibility for HIC is broader in scope.

Annex 4

Intelligence-led Security (IGV) [29]

The police and municipality each have their own 'Intelligence-led approach', on the basis of which the Intelligence-led Security was established wherein the direct input and participation of citizens and institutions plays an important role. With regard to the police, Intelligence-led Security is based on scientific knowledge about **'what does/does not work'** when it comes to security concerns. After studying a large number of publications from home and abroad, **three security strategies appeared to be effective**:

(1)   **Problem Oriented Policing** (POP) (Braga, 2002)

(2)   **Community-Oriented Policing** (COP)

(3)   **Intelligence-Led Policing** (ILP) [30]

The former Haaglanden police force therefore referred to the Intelligence-led Security as **'The Best of Three Worlds'**
www.politieacademie.nl/kennisenonderzoek/kennis/
mediatheek/PDF/78206.pdf.

▉▉ POP

The success of Problem-Oriented Policing is mainly due to the joint approach to the most important safety problems by all the security partners involved. An appropriate combination of preventive and punitive measures is implemented for each safety concern. Such a problem-oriented approach is based on an in-depth problem analysis, which examines the role that perpetrators, victims and environmental factors played in the origin of the problem.

---

[29] Politieacademie, 2014, https://thesaurus.politieacademie.nl/Thesaurus/Term/5117.

[30] In the Netherlands, we are familiar with the comparable National Intelligence Model (NIM): https://netpol.org/wp-content/uploads/2014/06/National-Intelligence-Model.pdf. In the Netherlands, the focus is on information, data, technology and advanced forms of data analysis. In the NIM, there is a lot more attention for the management process of 'setting tasks & coordinating' and the role of partners.

■■■ COP

The effectiveness of Community Policing – a subject that is also being addressed within CCI (see www.cuttingcrimeimpact.eu) – can mainly be attributed to the great involvement of citizens in concerns about safety, whereby information about the most important local problems and the wishes and expectations of neighbourhood residents help to determine local priorities.

■■■ ILP

The positive contribution to the security through Intelligence-Led Policing can mainly be attributed to the coordinated deployment of the police based on analysed information and knowledge (intelligence), result-oriented management by the police heads (accountability) and increasing the capacity for learning *(Ratcliffe, 2016)*.

Scientific discussions about which security strategy works best are still ongoing. It seems that the most scientific consensus is on the effectiveness of **POP**.[31]

MORE INFORMATION

Lam, et al, 2017; www.politieacademie.nl/ actueel/Documents/onderzoek%20aanpak%20 woninginbraken.pdf

Also see the video: www.youtube.com/ watch?v=gTuPQmK8dFo

---

[31] See the recent review (Knowledge Pearl 42*; Problem-Oriented Policing in England and Wales, 2019). An interesting finding is that POP is mainly a concern for the police: "little was said about the importance of and mechanisms for working with partners when problem-solving." See Problem Oriented Policing *(Sidebottom et al., 2019)*.

* More information about sources, see the digital version at **www.prohic.nl**

Annex 5

Citizen Participation Manuals

Manuals are chiefly written for **municipalities** and occasionally for the **police**.

An example of a manual for **municipalities** is the Association of Netherlands Municipalities publication *'Naar buiten: een spoorboekje burgerparticipatie voor raad en college'* from 2010. This includes a participation ladder with five different roles that citizens may play in the development and implementation of municipal policy: Self-Organisation, Co-decision, Co-production, Advising and Consulting (Association of Netherlands Municipalities & the Ministry of the Interior and Kingdom Relations, 2010). What is apparent, is that four of those roles relate to policy development and formulation, and only one of those five roles relates to the role that citizens play in policy implementation. This is typical of the role of the local government, since by far their most important task is to develop and determine policy.

For the **police**, there is a general overview www.politieacademie.nl/thema/ gebiedsgebondenpolitie/canonggp/ externesamenwerking/Paginas/ Burgerparticipatie.aspx available from the police academy.

The **police** manual 'Hot spot aanpak in vier stappen' *(Van Dijk et al., 2011)* includes an extensive section on citizen participation. A more recent example is a citizen participation manual www.dsp-groep. nl/wp-content/uploads/Menukaart-Burgerparticipatie-DSP-2015.pdf developed as part of a pilot project **'The Best of Three Worlds'** by the Noord-Holland police unit. These manuals place a greater emphasis on the role that citizens can play in carrying out concrete activities to make their home and/or their neighbourhood safer. This makes complete sense, as compared to the municipality, the police are an organisation that focuses much more on taking action and much less on policy.

This also explains why the municipality and the police often work at cross purposes when it comes to citizen participation, especially in neighbourhoods where there are serious problems. For example, a police project in the Schilderswijk in The Hague aimed at increasing the willingness of residents (often with an immigration background) to report crimes failed because the municipality had previously already set up a substantial citizen participation project carousel in the district *(Van Dijk et al., 2013)*.

As a result, people had difficulty absorbing this overabundance of information, and smart cooperation turned out to be impossible.

Annex 6

Involving citizens in decision-making

'Buurt bestuurt' is a well-known example www.rotterdam.nl/wonen-leven/buurt-bestuurt/.

The aim of this initiative is to find enough residents who are willing to work for the benefit of the neighbourhood. During the first meeting, they prioritise three topics that should be tackled first. Solutions can apply to everyone, or to a specific group: children, young people or the elderly, for example. A campaign or event is organised after establishing solid agreements and cooperation with each other. At a later stage, consultation about the result is important. For example, after a specific check, the police will provide feedback to the Neighbourhood Management Committee, e.g.: 'Forty fines issued for...'

We see that in practice, this form consequently combines the participation of citizens when it comes to how it is implemented. The question is whether this form of participation is also effective in tackling HIC. Ultimately, this depends on the measures that are implemented.

Annex 7

Prevention advice to citizens

Victims of residential burglaries (and their neighbours) need to be advised on the preventive measures that should be taken. After all, there is a reasonable chance of recurrence. Surprisingly, such a simple approach is hardly ever structurally organised in municipalities. For example, how easy would it be if the police - more specifically a detective and/or forensic assistant - not only looked at a case (burglary/armed robbery/ mugging) in terms of the investigation, but also provided preventive tips to the victim and their neighbours. The chance that a burglar will return to the victim's residence, or to the neighbours, is demonstrably present. See also the research on repeat victimisation.

The police can give these tips themselves, although a prevention training course may be more effective. The police could also have the prevention work be carried out by Victim Support Netherlands.[32] However, there are many other activities by the municipality, police and housing associations that can encourage citizens to take measures aimed at reducing the risk of burglary. These measures of an Organisational, Architectural and Electronic nature, referred to simply as OAE measures. A number of these measures have been proven to be effective. More prevention tips www. politiekeurmerk.nl/preventietips/. Also see the example of the Police Label Safe and Secure Housing.

---

[32] What few people know is that there is an EU directive from 2012 that mandates the provision of advice on the risk and prevention of repeat victimisation (article 8, 12, 18, 26). Article 8 sees a role for victims support organisations in this regard, unless this is provided for in some other way. Also see: DIRECTIVE 2012/29/EU OF THE EUROPEAN PARLIAMENT AND OF THE COUNCIL of 25 October 2012.

Annex 8

Neighbourhood Watch and Report Crime Anonymously

The original form of neighbourhood watch can be traced back to projects that were set up in the Netherlands as early as the 1980s. The 1990s saw the dawn of digital citizen networks, now known as the 'WhatsApp neighbourhood watch'.

The amount of research that has been done into neighbourhood security chat groups gives a somewhat mixed picture about their effectiveness *(Zoutendijk, 2019)*.

Burgernet

An app with almost three million participants, in which a participant receives a voice/text message or email when something happens in their direct environment. This message or email is usually a request to look out for a particular person or vehicle. Did you see something? Then make a quick call or send a message. www.burgernet.nl/app-info.

Burgernet is used for cases such as theft or break-ins, driving on after a collision, robbery and missing persons. The Burgernet Evaluation, which can be considered the first evaluation of new methods involving citizens in investigations, gives a good sense of the project's success:

66 *Nine municipalities in five police regions took part in the pilot. At the end of the pilot, there were almost 25,000 people participating in Burgernet. 4.6% of residents of the participating municipalities registered for Burgernet. A total of 192 case actions were carried out*

by the police during the pilot period. In 80 cases (41%) a successful detection was achieved. Some of these were not a direct result of Burgernet information. In 33 cases (17%), information was received from citizens and the cases were solved successfully. In eighteen cases (9%), a hard relationship can be established between the information received and the results from investigations. **99**

Van der Vijver et al., 2009

Positive results were already achieved with Burgernet during the experimental stage. Recent studies show that the use of the Burgernet app no longer leads to solving cases successfully. One obvious explanation is that, during the pilot phase, the police made much more of an effort to take targeted action to track down perpetrators based on the Burgernet information. The enormous growth to three million participants has probably contributed to the fact that the focus is now much more on finding missing persons. Over time, the goals have shifted and certain past results have proven to be unsustainable.

Report Crime Anonymously (Meld Misdaad Anoniem) is the independent reporting centre where anyone can provide anonymous information about crime, including murder, assault, armed robbery, drug abuse, arson and weapons /human trafficking. In 2019, the Report Crime Anonymously initiative *(Blauw Research, 2003)* was responsible for a total of 16,890 reports to the police and other investigative authorities. Feedback from the police in 2019 shows that at least 2,210 arrests were made, in part thanks to these tips. The Report Crime Anonymously initiative is active throughout the country, but there is also special attention for local campaigns (tailored approach) with, for example, interactive workshops for neighbourhood professionals, or by collaborating with self-help organisations or distributing target group-oriented campaign material.

 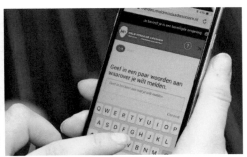

Also see the 2019 campaign aimed at young people (and HIC):
https://hetccv.nl/fileadmin/user_upload/220828_Infosheet_HIC.pdf.

Source photos:
Report Crime Anonymously
(Meld Misdaad Anoniem)

Annex 9

SARA Model

S
Scanning

- Identifying recurring problems of concern to the public and the police.
- Identifying the consequences of the problem for the community and the police.
- Prioritizing those problems.

- Developing broad goals.
- Confirming that the problems exist.
- Determining how frequently the problem occurs and how long it has been taking place.
- Selecting problems for closer examination.

A
Analysis

- Identifying and understanding the events and conditions that precede and accompany the problem.
- Identifying relevant data to be collected.
- Researching what is known about the problem type.
- Taking inventory of how the problem is currently addressed and the strengths and limitations of the current response.

- Narrowing the scope of the problem as specifically as possible.
- Identifying a variety of resources that may be of assistance in developing a deeper understanding of the problem.
- Developing a working hypothesis about why the problem is occurring.

R
Responses

- Brainstorming for new interventions.
- Searching for what other communities with similar problems have done.
- Choosing among the alternative interventions.

- Outlining a response plan and identifying responsible parties.
- Stating the specific objectives for the response plan.
- Carrying out the planned activities.

A
Assessment

- Determining whether the plan was implemented (a process evaluation).
- Collecting pre and post response qualitative and quantitative data.
- Determining whether broad goals and specific objectives were attained.

- Identifying any new strategies needed to augment the original plan.
- Conducting ongoing assessment to ensure continued effectiveness.

Annex 10

Area Scan and Hot Spot Map

During an area scan, field police officers, together with community police analysts, take a closer look at the police security analyses in a special meeting in order to gain insight into the main crime problems (concentrations) and the 'truth behind the figures'. The most persistent problems in the field of crime and trouble spots are mapped on an area level (district, neighbourhood) according to a standardised method. To this end, the so-called 'hard information' (system knowledge) is linked to 'soft information' and 'street knowledge', the latter two which are knowledge that community officers, patrol officers, detectives, youth police officers and other police officers contribute.

Police officers who work in these areas possess knowledge and information that cannot be obtained from systems. It is these police officers on the street who often identify developments at an early stage and who know the backgrounds of both their work areas and of the local residents/businesses. The area scan thus provides insight into the most important hot spots of crime and trouble spots in a certain area. Possible explanatory factors are also presented as to why a particular type of crime is concentrated in exactly that area. Using the area scan, the entire police force - from management to street officers - become involved in a problem-oriented approach for the most important problems in districts and neighbourhoods. It is important that the police - in light of their scanning and advisory roles - discuss the area scan at the earliest possible stage with the local triangle. Under the responsibility of the mayor, a meeting can then be held with the safety partners, in which the content of the area scan is discussed. Any (draft) plans stemming from the municipality and the Public Prosecutor can be addressed at the same time. This meeting is aimed at joint coordination of the planning of the police, the Public Prosecution Service, the municipality and, if needed, other organisations for the following calendar year. The results of the are scan and consultation thereof with the safety partners are then incorporated into the municipality's local safety plan for the following calendar year (see IVB).

FOR MORE INFORMATION, SEE:
www.politieacademie.nl/thema/gebiedsgebon-denpolitie/Documents/Gebiedsscan%20Crimi-naliteit%20en%20Overlast.pdf
And: https://hetccv.nl/onderwerpen/high-im-pact-crimes/HIC-preventiewijzer/geweld/geb-iedsscan-criminaliteit-en-overlast/

And: www.politieacademie.nl/kennisenonder-zoek/kennis/mediatheek/PDF/90501.PDF

BETREFT GEBIEDSSCAN VAN:

wrkgb NP: Basisteam Gouda

	DP: 2017	DP: 2018	DP: 2019	Verschil Jaar	Verschil Jaar %	Vorig Jaar	Dit Jaar	Verschil
High Impact Crime	620	493	366	-127	-26%	185	185	0
1.1.1. Diefstal/inbraak woning	596	475	348	-127	-27%	173	181	8
1.4.6. Straatroof	16	10	16	6	60%	10	3	-7
1.4.7. Overval	8	8	2	-6	-75%	2	1	-1

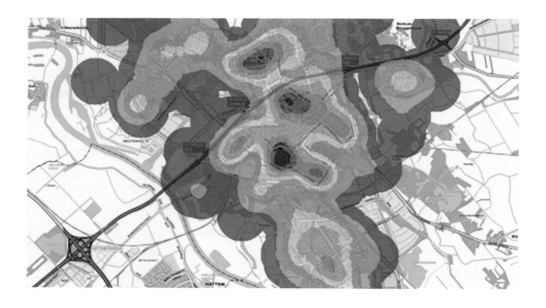

Annex 11

Crime Anticipation System (CAS)

Within Intelligence-led Policing there is also place for the CAS - the Crime Anticipation System - which is available in every Local Policing Unit and which is developed on the basis of a statistical model. In addition to information from the police, data used in the model also contains demographic and socio-economic facets. A map shows the areas with the highest statistical probability of a selection of common crimes, such as residential burglaries.

CAS is a form of Predictive Policing. This is a term that has come from the United States and was first used in 2008 in the Los Angeles Police Department. There are quite a few different definitions and interpretations of Predictive Policing. The Rand Corporation *(Perry et al., 2013)* states that

 predictive policing is the application of analytical techniques – particularly quantitative techniques – to identify likely targets for police intervention and prevent crime or solve past crimes by making statistical predictions. **99**

Predictive Policing is limited to the police force (likely targets for police interventions): police data in $\longrightarrow$ police action out.

The word 'predictive' is - certainly in the Netherlands - sometimes interpreted as a 'sure bet', even though it is, of course, an estimate or a probability calculation. A bit like the weather forecast, for example. Perry therefore states: likely (!) targets/statistical predictions.

CAS has been extensively and critically examined in various studies by the Police Academy *(Mali et al., 2017; Dubbeld, 2017)*, during research within the framework of the CCI *(Querbach et al., 2019)* and in studies by the Scientific Council for Government Policy *(WRR, 2016)*. For more information, see also Knowledge Pearl 5*.

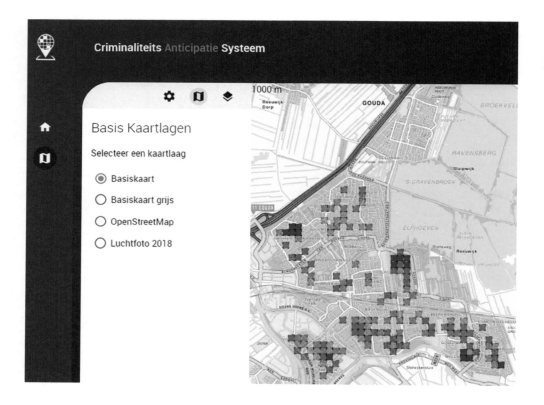

Annex 12

General Data Protection Regulation (GDPR)

Basic Principles of the GDPR (The Netherlands: AVG)

Based on the regulation, any processing of personal data must comply with the following principles:

- the processing of personal data must be lawful, proper and transparent ('Legitimacy, propriety and transparency');

- the processing must be linked to specific collection purposes ('purpose binding'); Purpose and purpose binding.

Personal data may in principle only be used for the specific purpose of the research and not for other purposes. This purpose must be clearly defined and explained to all parties involved:

- the personal data must be sufficient, relevant and limited to what is necessary ('minimum data processing'); Prevention is better than cure. Therefore, consider carefully which personal data is necessary for your research. By not collecting more than is strictly necessary (data minimisation), you reduce the risk to privacy. By dividing data over different files, you can also considerably reduce any risks to privacy;

- the data must be accurate ('accuracy');

- the data may not be kept longer than necessary ('storage limitation'); any Identifying data should be discarded as soon as it is no longer required for processing purposes.

- data must be properly secured and remain confidential ('integrity and confidentiality').

Data management: includes creating, storing, securing, maintaining, making available, archiving and long-term preservation of research data. Data management is essential for the quality, security, confidentiality and transparency of the research.

Processing Register

As a research agency, one is obliged to keep records of all processing of personal data in a registry. This is done during a process research registry*.

The Processing of Police Data

The Public Prosecutor, police, Royal Marechaussee, special investigative services and special investigating officers all process a multitude of data as part of their duties. The Dutch Act on Judicial and Prosecutorial Data (Wet justitiële en strafvorderlijke gegevens, Wjsg) and the Police Data Act (Wet politiegegevens, Wpg) include the option of providing this data to a third party when they require them for conducting scientific or statistical research or for obtaining policy information. Depending on the situation, the mayor, the Board of Prosecutors General or the Minister of Justice and Security are authorised to give permission for this. There are, however, requirements attached to such a provision. The requirements are considerably stricter concerning criminal law and police data that is processed in the context of investigations than when it is data that is processed in the context of day-to-day police or support tasks.

First read the manual on the Dutch Act on Judicial and Prosecutorial Data and Police Data Act data for scientific research, statistics and policy information. Manual for the Processors of Personal Data, General Data Protection Regulation (ou.nl) This way you can get an idea of the conditions and information that is requested. These concern:

- Information about the setup of the study.

- Information regarding the legal terms.

- The practical consequences of granting it.

Annex 13

Weighing up the seriousness of HIC

The question of how to measure crime has also been under consideration internationally for a long time already. In 1964, Marvin Wolfgang and Thorsten Sellin published their classic The measurement of delinquency https://journals.sagepub.com.

More recently (2020), a group of criminologists, statisticians and (former) police chiefs presented the Cambridge Harm Index Consensus *(Sherman et al., 2020)*:

66 *Crime statistics require a radical transformation if they are to provide transparent information for the general public, as well as police operational decision-making. This statement provides a blueprint for such a transformation.* 99

MORE INFORMATION
in Knowledge Pearl 50[*]

We take a similar approach here in order to weigh up the seriousness of a crime:

Firstly, we look at the (average) cost of HIC. International research shows that an armed robbery costs approximately twice the cost of a residential burglary *(Van Soomeren & Wever, 2015)*. It is important to remember that this is an average, and locally these costs may differ significantly.

Secondly - and perhaps better still - we can look at the types of punishment. For example, society considers a criminal offence with an average prison sentence of two years twice as serious as an offence with only a one-year sentence. The exact sentence varies from case to case. Ultimately, the punishment is always dependent on a number of factors, such as the level of violence, recidivism, number of people involved, etc. But if we look at punitive measures, a residential burglary generally means about three months in prison and a street robbery six to fifteen months.[33] An armed robbery of a shop results in 24 months and a residential robbery gets 36 months; threatening a shopkeeper or resident will add another year. Conversion into a single figure is always difficult, and cases may even differ from location to location, but our analysis shows:

	Sentence in months	Gravity of the crime
Residential burglary	3	1
(Armed) robbery	42	14
Street robbery	15	5

In a municipality of approximately 170,000 residents, which is a fairly exact reflection of The Netherlands, but where disproportionately a lot of armed robberies take place in homes and companies/shops, we are able to take the following figures as an example:

Criminal offence	Number	Seriousness of the crime	Number x gravity
Woninginbraak	395	1	395
Overval	23	14	322
Straatroof	4	5	20

While there is a disproportionately high number of armed robberies here, we see in this example that - due to the large number - break-ins/burglaries still score highest in the seriousness column.

It is important to remember here that safety is partly a subjective concept. For example, see the brochure about CCI instrument 'Perception matters' www. cuttingcrimeimpact.eu/imagem/Perception%20Matters.pdf.

---

[33] See www.rechtspraak.nl; Oriëntatiepunten voor straftoemeting en LOVS afspraken maart 2020. For more information see: OM-Richtlijnenbundel, Versie 0.12, januari 2020.

Annex 14

Funnel effect

The police are well aware of the vast majority of residential burglaries, street robberies and armed robberies (HIC) that take place. That is because almost everyone who becomes a victim of these crimes reports them to the police (or is required to by their insurance company). This is less the case for many other types of crimes. According to Statistics Netherlands (2019), only one third of all violence to property and vandalism crimes combined were reported to the police in 2019.[34] Moreover, an official report was only actually filed for one quarter (23 percent) of these criminal offences.

This is also referred to as the 'funnel effect': only a part of all crime is reported to the police and only a part thereof ends up with an official police report being registered. This funnel effect then merely continues. Of the reported crimes, only a very small section is solved and only a few perpetrator(s) are caught. Of all known perpetrators, the Public Prosecutor ultimately just brings a few to court via a summons, of which only some of them are eventually sentenced.

The overall picture is as follows:

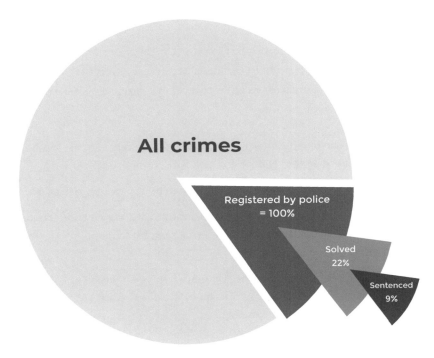

All crimes

Registered by police
= 100%

Solved
22%

Sentenced
9%

---

34 In 2019, 14 percent was reported via an official charge; 9 percent via the internet.

Here, it is not so much about the exact figures, but more about the effect. In addition, the more serious crimes there are, the greater the chance of remaining in the funnel: people generally only go to the police with more serious cases, the most serious of which then go before the Public Prosecutor and the judge. The serious crimes are right in the middle of the whirlpool and end at the funnel mouth. The best example is murder: it is almost always reported to the police, who then invest a lot of resources into solving it. Once the perpetrator is known[35], they will be brought to court and almost always convicted. From the perspective of criminal law, this is a positive thing: perpetrators do end up paying for their crimes. It is more difficult for the analyst/researcher, however, because the further down the funnel you descend, the more selective the data becomes. Police records consequently paint a 'too serious' picture of crime (see the slice of the pie) and for the justice department, it is even 'more serious'. In research jargon, this is referred to as a bias: the data does not accurately reflect reality.

Annex 15

Triangulation

Triangulation is an approach from social sciences, in which it is assumed that combining multiple observers, theories, methods and empirical materials leads to better analysis results. There are four types of triangulations:

- **Data**: use of different sources (police, municipality, Public Prosecution Service, Statistics Netherlands, citizens/businesses).

- **Analysts**: two or more analysts/researchers know more than one.

- **Theory**: formulate more ideas about the 'why'. Which criminogenic and protective factors play a role with regard to perpetrators, victims and location.

- **Methods and techniques**: use more than one method to collect data: e.g., interviews, observations, questionnaires, images (photo, vlogs[36]), social media and documents.

---

[35] Murders are usually solved, especially because they often concern a delict in the relational context: in many cases, a close acquaintance or partner is the perpetrator. And where this is not the case, the butler did it. Case solved.

[36] These can also be made by residents, for example. Also see Example Noord.

Annex 16

Ideas about joint surveys

▰▰▰ Joint surveys[37]

In England, this approach was once formulated and adopted under the name: *Crime Opportunity Profiling of Streets*.[38] This approach falls within the long and broad tradition of CPTED (Crime Prevention Through Environmental Design; www.CPTED.net) or what is known as 'Veilig Ontwerp en Beheer' in the Netherlands (www.SVOB.nl and *Luten, 2008*).[39]

The approach is simple, practical, acts as a catalyst for better contacts/relationships with other stakeholders, provides a good and fast overview of problems and leads to very concrete and measurable sets of goals and results. A credible example of a page from a joint survey list (can be immediately entered into an app) is as follows:

Parking garage 25

Details
Address: Van Damenstraat 140, 1043 AB
Amsterdam, The Netherlands
Type of building: Public parking garage
Owner/victim: Paul van Dijk – manager
Van Damenstraat 120, 1043 AC Amsterdam,
020 625 34 34

Problem
Drug users always have access to the parking garage. They leave used needles and other drug paraphernalia in the parking garage and are responsible for many of the thefts from motor vehicles. There is no entrance control to the car park and many spaces in the car park are used by homeless people and drug abusers.

Recommendations/approach
In essence: the car park needs to have an entrance control system that is operated via parking tickets. Advice has been given to the owner to upgrade the garage/car park and to have people park according to ACPO's secure car park standards. See report Park 345 AA for a full list of recommendations.

Person in charge who pushes everything through: Armando de Krom, National Police Netherlands

---

[37] See Knowledge Pearl 29* and also step 10 from the 60 steps: https://popcenter.asu.edu/sites/default/files/library/reading/PDFs/60steps_dutch.pdf.

[38] www.dsp-groep.nl/wp-content/uploads/COPS_16_COPS_guide.pdf.

[39] Also see chapter 9 in the Basisboek Integrale Veiligheid, Boom Criminologie Den Haag, 2016, p. 141-154 and see www.svob.nl. In the CCI project (www.cuttingcrimeimpact.eu) they talk about CP-UDP: Crime Prevention through Urban Design and Planning. Since 2021, there is a global standard for CPTED: ISO 22431:2021.

* More information about sources, see the digital version at www.prohic.nl

Annex 17

Analysis and Approach to Youth Networks

◼◼◼ Problem-oriented approach

In 2012 , the municipality of The Hague had to contend with youth networks that were responsible for an increase in crime and causing trouble in the operational area of the Beresteinlaan police station. In this case, it mainly concerned the Bouwlust, Vrederust and Wateringseveld neighbourhoods within the Escamp district of The Hague. In 2013, the Beresteinlaan police station actively started working with various partners on a problem-oriented approach.

The Crime and Nuisance Beresteinlaan area scan 2012 was used as an initial exploration of the problems surrounding incidents of residential burglaries and nuisance. The area scan also showed that certain *hot groups* were active in certain *hot spots*.

◼◼◼ Qualitative research

To get a better idea of the situation in the neighbourhood, the police commissioned a (largely) qualitative study *(De Jong, 2012)*. The analysis in this study was structured according to the crime triangle: perpetrators, victims and environmental factors (**Annex 21**).

The research showed that among the boys of these criminal youth networks, there was a (street) culture in which people had to prove themselves that they 'belonged'. Moreover, feelings of being left out formed legitimacy for criminal activities. De Jong notes that the victims of residential burglaries by youth networks are diverse and that there is no clear prototype victim. However, he did mention the decline in contact between residents and youth groups on the street as a factor that contributes to the youths 'living outside of society.' With regard to environmental factors, De Jong refers to the 'degradation' of the neighbourhoods and the lack of preventive measures in homes which invariably make it easy for burglars to target certain homes.

De Jong makes recommendations for a problem-oriented approach based on the environmental factors, background problems and street culture existing among these youth groups. These can be divided into repression, prevention and civic participation. Repression must ensure that the criminal leaders can be better identified and dealt with more harshly. Preventive measures contribute to good support for young people in these areas and should offer them opportunities for a better future. Furthermore, increasing civic participation can restore public confidence in government and the police. This can be achieved through social contacts between neighbourhood police officers, residents and youth groups. More personal contact increases social control and a sense of engagement and lowers feelings of anxiety.

Tactical perpetrator group analysis

A so-called *Tactical Perpetrator Group Analysis* was of great importance in tackling crime and nuisance by youth networks in the Beresteinlaan operating area. This analysis consists of structuring and comparing the data that is available about a particular perpetrator (group). This is how more insight can be gained into a criminal group and each individual's part in illegal activities can be discerned.

In Bouwlust-Vrederust, for example, together with community police officers and detectives, it was established which youths are part of the criminal youth network. This analysis revealed that 72 youths were responsible for at least 177 residential burglaries, 68 assaults, 37 threats, 45 aggravated robberies, 31 simple thefts, 25 vandalism cases and 16 insults against civil servants. A distinction could also be made between different types of members within the criminal youth network. For example, there was a more serious target group of criminal leaders and ambitious delinquents (in total about 25 youths). They are actively committing acts of crime. There is also a more marginal target group consisting of followers, non-criminals and facilitators. They do not commit crimes directly, but mainly perform supporting tasks, such as distracting the police, providing information and providing a sales market for stolen items.

Identification of perpetrators: Spectra and Hit Team

Based on these analyses, it was decided to adopt a broad approach to the problem in the neighbourhood, whereby the police, the municipality (OOV and compulsory education), the Public Prosecution Service, the Youth Care Agency, the Netherlands Probation Service and youth work groups all worked together. Residents and shop owners were also involved.

The measures taken can be divided as follows:

- Perpetrator-oriented measures (both punitive and preventive), focusing on the investigation and prosecution of criminals within the youth networks, but also measures such as camera surveillance, hot spot surveillance and area bans.

- In addition, victim-oriented measures were also implemented, such as informing and advising residents and the police promoting burglary prevention.

However, the emphasis in the approach was on tracking down perpetrators.

The Spectra research team was established at the end of February 2013. This team of ten employees took a criminal justice approach to tackling the criminal youth network. The Tactical Perpetrator Group Analysis provided a clear focus here. The Spectra team mainly focused on the criminal leaders and ambitious delinquents within the criminal youth network: Perpetrators previously described as rising stars or up-and-coming talent (see the Example: Tackling Hot Shots).

When the Spectra team got to work at the end of February, a good system of information management for the team was arranged first. The team members were given courses on how to work with a special investigation information application (SUMM-IT). Moreover, the identification of all members of the criminal youth network was also entered into the Police and Law Enforcement Database (BVH). This allows the Spectra team to be informed as soon as members of the network were apprehended elsewhere in the city or country. Once the information management system was properly arranged, the 'real' work could commence. To get things up and running properly, the detectives first needed information about the criminal youth network. To do this, the project leader mobilised the already existing Hot Spot Intervention Team (HIT team). The HIT team comprises four patrol officers who are fully dedicated to targeted surveillance at the hot spots for residential burglaries and juvenile delinquency. This team therefore had access to street information that was important for the investigation. The HIT team was placed under the project manager of the Spectra team. From then on, the HIT team monitored the members of the criminal youth network, collected information about them (who is accompanying who, what car are they driving, what clothes are they wearing, etc.) and subsequently checked them according to the BAND principle ('Bekeuren, Aanhouden, Noteren, Doorgeven': Fine, Detain, Note, Pass on). All this information was passed on to the Spectra team. The Spectra team set to work with this information and tried to bring cases against the members of the network.

Results

One of the key objectives of this problem-oriented approach was to reduce the number of residential burglaries and nuisance reports *(Terpstra & Van Dijk, 2014)*. This was further quantified by the Spectra team, which set a target for a 20% reduction in residential burglaries and nuisance reports in the form of an action plan. It is important to compare the results of the problem-oriented approach with other developments in the city and district. This allows concrete judgements to be made about the effectiveness of the measures that had been taken.

We can see that in 2013, residential burglaries in the whole of The Hague were reduced by 13%, while there was a reduction of 23% in the Escamp district. In the Beresteinlaan project area, the number of residential burglaries dropped by 22%, which means that the Spectra team's objective was achieved. The number of reports of nuisance incidents in the project area dropped by 17%, which means that the target was not quite achieved. However, this reduction is many times greater than in other parts of the Escamp district, where a reduction of just 6% took place. The problem-oriented approach was strongly focused on the Bouwlust-Vrederust neighbourhoods. Here, there was clearly a greater decline in residential burglaries (- 28% compared to - 8%) and nuisance reports (- 20% compared to - 10%) than in the adjacent Wateringseveld neighbourhood. The project has shown that internal cooperation within the police, such as cooperation between investigative officers and enforcement officers, can lead to success. politie, zoals de samenwerking tussen opsporing en handhaving, tot succes kan leiden.

Annex 18

Knowledge Databases

There are several databases for interventions in the social domain. If an intervention is to be considered eligible for assessment and a registered inclusion in a database, the intervention must be registered and described in a specially designed worksheet. The sections in this worksheet follow the accreditation criteria set out by the committee. A manual is also available with this worksheet.

MORE INFORMATION

www.justitieleinterventies.nl/erkenningstraject

(worksheet description intervention + manual worksheet description intervention).

Database	Theme	Knowledge institute
Database Effective Youth Interventions	Youth care and promotion of development	Netherlands Youth Institute
Database Gezond en Actief Leven (Database Healthy and Active Life)	Health promotion	National Institute for Public Health and the Environment/Centrum Gezond Leven
Interventions Library	Youth health care and prevention	Netherlands Youth Health Centre
Sports and Exercise Interventions	Sports and exercise	Knowledge Centre Sports & Exercise
Department of Justice Interventions	Department of Justice Interventions	Dutch Youth Institute, Movisie, Trimbos Institute
Databank Effective Social Interventions	Well-being, participation, social care	Movisie
Long-term Care Database	Long-term care for the elderly and disabled	Vilans

These kinds of databases often concern more extensive interventions. It is often a combination of measures and resources known as a 'mechanism' in the terminology of Ray Pawson and Nick Tilley *(Pawson & Tilley, 1997)*. In their view, it is always about a combination of the trio C-M-O: Context - Mechanism - Outcome. Every context needs a set of smart measures to accomplish the desired outcome. The CMO principle is popular with the Scientific Research and Documentation Centre (Wetenschappelijk Onderzoek- en Documentatie Centrum, WODC) of the Dutch Ministry of Justice and Security and is therefore often encountered in WODC evaluations. Other terms include 'policy theory', 'goal-resources chain' or 'goal tree' (a Christmas tree with at the top, the main goal followed by a few other goals, several sub-goals (and sometimes sub-sub-goals) and at the bottom a large number of measures and resources). Also see section 5.1 in this Book of Basics.

Annex 19

The Two Dimensions of the Crime Matrix

This idea for a matrix was formulated in 1991 by Jan van Dijk en Jaap de Waard and has been widely applied ever since.[40] In this model the authors combine the well-known threefold division that was later also part of the 'crime triangle' (see section 4.2 in this Book of Basics) with a threefold division that originated from medical science (in particular preventive medical science). This is where primary, secondary and tertiary approaches are referred to.

In a **primary** approach, actions are aimed at the whole population. Clean water and good sewage systems are typical examples of this. They are examples of primarily preventive measures that are taken by others ([urban] planners and engineers) without the involvement of medical experts, but which often stem

[40] For example, see chapter 6 about Crime Prevention in the 'Actuele Criminologie' textbook' *(Van Dijk et al., 2006)*.

from the latter's recommendations and research.[41] All efforts to influence people's behaviour towards a healthier lifestyle also fall under this, referred to as the Big Five: Exercise, Smoking, Alcohol, Nutrition, Safety and lastly, Leisure *(Van der Velpen, 2018)*. General public information about the problem-oriented approach to HIC and, for example, the inclusion of an article about burglary-proof measures in the regulations of the Dutch Building Decree and the Police Label Safe and Secure Housing are good examples in the HIC sphere.

The **Secondary** approach focuses on risk groups who sometimes already show initial symptoms of a disease, or who are at a much greater risk of developing the disease in question. For example, think of people who have worked with asbestos, or in the mines (pneumoconiosis), or pay attention to salt in diets for people who have high blood pressure, or tackling AIDS prevention among homosexuals and prostitutes. A great deal of research and

analysis is required in order to find out exactly which groups are at risk. Once you know where the risk groups are located, a much more efficient implementation of measures will be possible. However, this often creates ethical problems too (look at the example of AIDS). With regard to HIC, the Top 600 approach and the tackling of (criminal) youth networks are good examples (see Example Tackling Hot Shots and Berensteinlaan).

A **Tertiary** approach focuses on people who are already sick and who you want to prevent from developing complications, and preferably you want them do get better and stay that way. As far as HIC is concerned, we can think of punitive measures and reducing recidivism. Combining these dimensions produces a matrix with nine boxes in which all of the measures can be arranged in order. This may involve preventive, but also reactive/repressive measures.

	Perpetrator	Victim	Situation/Environment/Time
Primary (whole municipality and everyone)			
Secondary (risk groups and areas)			
Tertiary (real core and risk groups/areas)			

See page 65 of https://eucpn.org/sites/default/files/document/files/brochure_domestic_burglary_gb_3.pdf about burglaries in Europe.

[41] For instance, the surgeon John Snow (1813-1858) showed that a person can get cholera from water contaminated by waste from other cholera patients. He demonstrated this through what we would today call a hot spot analysis and published his theory in the mid-nineteenth century under the title *'On the Mode of Communication of Cholera'*. This detailed hot spot analysis of the impact of water supply on the 1854 London cholera outbreak (including a detailed map featuring the hot spots) spurred the development of better sewage systems and water supply.

Annex 20

Simple Process Evaluation Form (PEF)

Date	
Project name/code	
Period that we are reporting on	
Project budget	
Participants	
Municipality/neighbourhoods	

A. GENERAL		
1	Form completed by:	
2	With the assistance of -internal: -external:	
3	Commissioning party (contact person triangle):	
4	More info available (report, files, links):	
5	Was it realised within the planned timeframe and budget?	
6	Any time delays/excess money spent caused by:	
7	(Un)foreseen amounts of/extra time/ money spent on:	

B. EVALUATION (process)		
10	How did the process go (what went well/less well):	
11	What would you do differently next time?	
12	Reactions from others (triangle, residents, press) about the process (informal and as far as known):	

C. EFFECT		
	Are the effects known? Have the goals been achieved?	
8	Unexpected results (both positive and negative effects):	
9	Can anything be said about the wider social consequences/effects of the project?	

Annex 21

Possible Questions for the Process Evaluation

Based on the literature *(o.a. Pawson & Tilley, 2004 en Shaw et al., 2006)* and our own experiences, we have put together the following checklist. The list contains all questions that could be answered in either a narrow (n) or a broad (b) process evaluation. In total, the list contains more than 100 questions. Answering all the questions is therefore impractical. However, the list is intended to provide you with ideas and/or an opportunity to select the best questions. Tick the questions that really must be answered (e.g., because others insist) and tick the questions you would like to see answered. In the final choice, the 'must' questions have first priority. Consider this list as a checklist, so that nothing is forgotten.[42] How the ticked questions are asked exactly and who they are put to is subsequently up to the evaluator.

You can, of course, also present the list to the target groups that you have identified for the process evaluation under the motto 'indicate what is very interesting (1), interesting (2), neutral (3), moderately interesting (4), or not interesting (5)'.

A. The project

	MUST be answered	WOULD LIKE to see answered
1. Goal analysis, resources and activities analysis (N/B)		
Where is the project area located (indicate the exact boundaries)?		
Characterisation of the project area according to size, number of residents, population structure, type of buildings or other relevant characteristics.		

---

[42] Questions are sometimes asked in the present tense and sometimes in the past tense. In a report after an event, people tend to look back, but when they ask a question, they tend to look forward.

Type of problem in the project area (problem to be tackled as part of the project).		
What were the (probable) causes of the problem that the project aims to address?		
Who suffered from the problem(s)?		
Which target group was the project focusing on (type, size)?		
What are the specific causes of the problems the target group had?		
Which measures have been applied to which problems and which target group?		
How did the project progress?		
How many people from the target group were contacted with regard to each individual measure or activity?		
How much did it cost per measure/ activity (money and man-hours)?		
Have the measures/project plan been adjusted in the interim? If yes, why?		
Have there been any sticking points? If so, which ones and what was learned from these?		
Did certain measures prove to be particularly effective? If so, which ones and what was learned from these?		
Have certain (groups of) measures not been implemented? If so, which ones and why not?		
Where is the project area located (indicate the exact boundaries)?		
Characterisation of the project area according to size, number of residents, population structure, type of buildings or other relevant characteristics.		

Type of problem in the project area (problem to be tackled as part of the project).		
What were the (probable) causes of the problem that the project aims to address?		
Who suffered from the problem(s)?		
Which target group was the project focusing on (type, size)?		
What are the specific causes of the problems the target group had?		
Which measures have been applied to which problems and which target group?		
How did the project progress?		
How many people from the target group were contacted about each individual measure or activity?		
2. Evaluation (N/B)		
How are the effects of the project measured? Are the output and/or outcome looked at? Impact?		
How are the processes within and around the project evaluated?		
Who evaluates (internally/externally) and who oversees the evaluation?		
Budget for evaluation (in hours and money)		
How is the independence of the evaluation safeguarded? What about privacy concerns (consent)?		
3. Extent of change required (B)		
To what extent was the target group required to change?		

To what extent was the policy of the organisations involved required to change?		
To what extent was change required from employees within the organisations involved?		
To what extent was change required of organisations in the environment where the project was carried out?		
Which organisations in the project's environment were affected by how the project was carried out?		
4. Sanctions (N/B)		
Who, within the project, was entitled to impose sanctions in order to make sure the project was being implemented? What kind of sanctions did they have at their disposal?		
5. Benefits (B)		
To what extent did the project address the needs of the target group?		
Did the project lead to better work results for the organisations involved?		
Was the project worth the time and energy that was invested in it?		
Has the project helped to better achieve the objectives of the individual organisations involved?		
Has the project met the needs of the organisations involved?		

	MUST be answered	WOULD LIKE to see answered
1. Preliminary decision-making process (B)		
Who are the initiators of the project?		
What are the motives and concerns of the initiators in implementing the project?		
Who are the decision makers who subsequently stood behind the project?		
To what extent did these decision-makers have direct power over those carrying out the project?		
Was there any research done on the problems beforehand?		
What sticking points arose during the preparation?		
2. Management processes/support base in organisation(s) (B)		
What was the role of the organisation(s) participating in the project in the decision to carry out the project?		
What was the role of the management or leadership of those organisations in the decision to carry out the project?		
How broad was the support base for the decision to proceed with the project amongst the part of the organisation(s) who were involved in implementing it?		
3. Resources (N/B)		
What was the size of the budget?		
What was/were the source(s) for funding the project?		

Was additional funding required (or could all costs be covered within the regular budget)? If so, where did this money come from?		
How many people were able to be assigned to the project (staff and hours)?		
Who provided these people?		
Was there a need for new employees?		
How big was the target group?		
Was it necessary to define a new target group? Which one? How big was this group?		
Characteristics of each target group.		
How much time did it take to prepare the short-term planning and what did it look like?		
How much time did it take to prepare the long-term planning and what did it look like?		
Was there a need for (re)training the staff who carried out the project?		
Who provided the training for the staff who carried out the project?		
Were additional facilities, buildings or space required? If yes, which ones?		
4. Role of the environment (B)		
Were any activities undertaken by the target group(s) that made it easier to implement the project? If so, what activities were these? (Possibly also which target group?)		
Were there any activities undertaken by the target group(s) that hindered the implementation of the project? If so, what activities were these? (Possibly also which target group?)		

Were there any activities on the part of the financiers that made it easier to implement the project? If so, what activities and where appropriate, which financier?		
Were there any activities on the part of the financiers that hindered the implementation of the project? If so, what activities and where appropriate, which financier?		
Was there a case of activities undertaken by other (competing) organisations that made the implementation of the project easier? If so, what activities and organisations were these?		
Was there a case of activities undertaken by other (competing) organisations that hindered the implementation of the project? If so, what activities and organisations were these?		
Were there any activities undertaken by regulatory authorities that made the implementation of the project easier? If so, what activities and organisations were these?		
Were there any activities undertaken by regulatory authorities that hindered the implementation of the project? If so, what activities and organisations were these?		
Were there any other agencies that made it easier to implement the project?		
Were there any other agencies that hindered the implementation of the project?		

5. Laws and regulations

Did any laws or regulations lead to changes in the setup of the project? If so, which laws and regulations were those? • What legal requirements did the project have to meet? • Which government schemes (e.g., subsidies) were relevant? • Which rules were drawn up for project employees (and possibly the target group)?		

6. Political environment		
How did public opinion regarding the project play out?		
How did the opinion of the municipal politics (or other political figures, e.g., the triangle) about the project develop?		
Which groups had an interest in the project and/or supported the project?		
How was the project reported in the media?		

C. People and organisational characteristics in the project

	MUST be answered	WOULD LIKE to see answered
1. Relationship between project coordinators and project staff (B)		
How many coordinators were there and (if more than one) how was the division of tasks between them?		
What is the education level of the prevention officer?		
How much experience did the prevention officer have (with coordination and in other positions)?		

Does the prevention officer have experience as a member of the target group?		
What is the age of the prevention officer?		
What is the prevention officer's gender?		
What is the prevention officer's ethnicity?		
What views of the prevention officer could have been important in the implementation of the project?		
Which methods should the prevention officer use?		
Who provided additional training for the prevention officer?		
What is the (average) level of education of the project staff?		
What level of experience does the the project staff have with similar projects?		
What kind of work experience did the project staff have?		
Did the project staff require any special training in order to carry out the project?		
Did project staff in any way benefit from the change in their duties?		
Was project staff in any way disadvantaged by the change in their duties?		
To what extent did the project staff have influence in setting up the project?		
To what extent did project staff make any adjustments to the project while it was being carried out?		
How many coordinators were there and (if more than one) how was the division of tasks between them?		

2. The role of routine procedures (B)		
What routine procedures (if relevant to the project) existed within participating organisations prior to the implementation of the project?		
What were the job descriptions of the regular day-to-day work of the staff (prior to the project)?		
How much time was required to teach the project staff their new tasks?		
3. Company culture (B) note: for each participating organisation		
To what extent did the project's working methods differ from the way in which the organisations normally work?		
To what extent was the project in line with the philosophy of the organisations?		
To what extent did the project match the priorities or focal points of the organisations?		
What influence did the project staff have during the implementation of the project?		
What was the attitude of the project staff towards the project?		
What attitude did those who were carrying out the project have towards it?		
Was there any resistance to the project among the project staff?		
Was there any resistance to the project among the staff carrying it out?		
Has staff turnover increased as a result of the project?		

Bibliography

All Knowledge Pearls referred to in this book can also be found on the website The Knowlede Pearls from Jaap de Waard - ProHIC.*

* More information about sources, see the digital version at www.prohic.nl

Abraham, M. & Van Soomeren, P. (2020). *Boa's: buitengewoon veilig. Onderzoek naar taken en arbeidsomstandigheden van boa's en de samenwerking met politie.* **Ministry of Justice and Security, WODC.**

Actieprogramma Lokale Besturing Politie. (2012). *Gemeentelijke Veiligheidszorg. Volop lokale kansen in nieuw politiebestel.* **Ministry of Justice and Security.** www.regioburgemeesters.nl/save113/

Altes, H.J., Stienstra, H., IJmker, A., Van Soomeren, P. & Van der Gugten, M. (1993). *Naar een Politiekeurmerk Veilig Wonen, voorstudie 'Secured by Design' in Nederland.* **DSP-groep.** www.dsp-groep.nl/wp-content/uploads/93_34_Naar-een-Politiekeurmerk-Veilig-Wonen_34-19932.pdf

Akkermans, M. & Kloosterman, R. (2020). *Veiligheidsbeleving van slachtoffers van criminaliteit. CBS Statistische Trends.* www.cbs.nl/nl-nl/longread/statistische-trends/2020/veiligheidsbeleving-van-slachtoffers-van-criminaliteit

Beckford, C., Kong, S., Whitworth, M. & Henson, N. (2003). *A practical and developing guide to help identify and deal with crime oppurtunity generators in the street environment.* **Annex-16-COPS: Crime Opportunity Profiling of Streets, a practical guide.** www.dsp-groep.nl/wp-content/uploads/COPS_16_COPS_guide.pdf

Beijersbergen, K.A., Blokdijk, D. & Weijters, G. (2018). *Recidive onder daders van high impact crimes veroordeeld in de periode 2002-2013.* **WODC.** www.wodc.nl/onderzoeksdatabase/2786b-recidive-na-een-high-impact-crime.aspx

Beke, B. Klein Hofmeijer, E. & Versteegh, P. (2008). **Gebiedsscan criminaliteit & overlast. Een methodiekbeschrijving.** *Politiekunde, 22.* **Arnhem.** www.politieenwetenschap.nl/publicatie/politiekunde/2008/gebiedsscan-criminaliteit-overlast-130/

Beke, B., Ferwerda, H., Bervoets, E. & Van der Torre, E. (2013). *Geweld van de straat? Jeugdgroepen en geweld. Van signalering naar aanpak.* **Boom Lemma.**

Benders, L. (2020). *Doelen formuleren met de SMART-methode.* www.scribbr.nl/modellen/smart-methode/

Berghuis, B. (2018). **Is de Top600 van Amsterdam een succes?** *In Secondant – Platform voor Maatschappelijke veiligheid.* https://ccv-secondant.nl/platform/article/is-de-top-600-van-amsterdam-een-succes

Beunders, H.J.G., Abraham, M.D., Van Dijk, A.G. & Van Hoek, A. (2011). *Een onderzoek naar de communicatievormen tussen burgers en blauw. Politiewetenschap 54.* https://www. politieenwetenschap.nl/publicatie/politiewetenschap/2011/politie-en-publiek-176/

Blauw Research BV. (2003). *Eindrapportage Evaluatie pilot M.* https://www.wodc.nl/binaries/ewb03mels-samenvatting_tcm28-67409.pdf

Boer, j. (2020). Wonen boven winkels. *NUL20, nr. 102 maart 2020.*

Braga, A.A. (2002). *Problem-Oriented Policing and Crime Prevention.* Criminal Justice Press.

Braga, A.A., Weisburd, D. & Turchan, B. (2019). Focused deterrence strategies effects on crime: A systematic review. *Campbell Systematic Reviews, vol. 15, no. 3, 1-65.* https:// onlinelibrary.wiley.com/doi/pdf/10.1002/cl2.1051

Bruinink, J.E. & Lagendijk, E.P. (1994). *Aanpak stelselmatige daders in Dordrecht: Een stok achter de deur! Inzoomstudie in het kader van het evaluatieonderzoek 'Buurtbeheer en criminaliteitspreventie'.* https://www.dsp-groep.nl/wp-content/uploads/94_06_Aanpak-stelselmatige-daders-in-Dordrecht-Een-stok-achter-de-deur_06-19942.pdf

Bruinink, J.E., Van der Gugten, M. & Van Soomeren, P.F. (1994). *Eindrapport Buurtbeheer en Criminaliteitspreventie in Dordrecht 1990 – 1993.* www.dsp-groep.nl/wp-content/ uploads/94_18_Eindrapport-Buurtbeheer-en-Criminaliteitspreventie-in-Dordrecht-1990-1993_18-1994.pdf (dsp-groep.nl)

CBS. (2013). *Veiligheidsmonitor 2012.*

CBS. (2014). *Veiligheidsmonitor 2013.*

CBS. (2015). *Veiligheidsmonitor 2014.*

CBS. (2019). *Slachtofferschap criminaliteit. Veiligheidsmonitor 2019.* https://longreads.cbs. nl/veiligheidsmonitor-2019/slachtofferschap-criminaliteit/

Chenery, S. & Pease, K. (2000). *The Burnley/Dordrecht Initiative Final Report.* University of Huddersfield/Safer Cities Partnership (unpublished).

Chito, J. (2001). *The role of local government in community safety. U.S.* Department of Justice Office of Justice Programs, Bureau of Justice Assistance. Washington DC, USA.

Clarke, R.V. & Eck, J.E. (2010). *Crime Analysis for Problem Solvers In 60 Small Steps.* https://popcenter.asu.edu/content/crime-analysis-problem-solvers-60-small-steps

Clarke, R.V. (1999). Hot Products. *Police Research Series. Paper 112.* London: Home Office. www.popcenter.org

Dawson, P. & Cuppleditch, L. (2007). *An impact assessment of the Prolific and other Priority Offender programme.*

De Jong, J.D.A. (2012). *Ons kent ons. Naar een probleemgerichte analyse van een crimineel (jeugd)netwerk.* Beresteinlaan Police Station, Rebond/Ministry of Justice and Security, Haaglanden Police, Analyse en Research.

Deetman, W.J. (1988). Macht en onmacht van evaluatie van en door bestuur. *Ringeling, A.B. & Sorber A. (1988). Macht en onmacht van bestuurlijke evaluaties. VUGA, Geschriften van de Vereniging van Bestuurskunde, nr 11.*

De Stercke, J., Liagre, F. & Stove, A. (2014). *An integral methodology to develop an information-led and community-orientated policy to tackle domestic burglary.* General Directorate Security and Prevention, Belgian Ministry of Internal Affairs. https://eucpn.org/sites/default/files/document/files/brochure_domestic_burglary_gb_3.pdf

Dubbeld, L. (2017). Predictive policing: Niet alleen een zaak van de politie. *Security Management, 9, p. 28-31.* www.politieacademie.nl/kennisenonderzoek/kennis/mediatheek/PDF/93870.PDF

Eck, J.E. (2010). Places and the Crime Triangle. *Encyclopedia of Criminological Theory (p. 281-285).* Thousand Oaks: SAGE Publications. https://sk.sagepub.com/reference/criminologicaltheory/n77.xml | https://study.sagepub.com/system/files/Eck%2C_John_E._-_Places_and_the_Crime_Triangle.pdf

Eck, J.E. & Spelman, W. (1987). *Problem-Solving: Problem-Oriented Policing in Newport News.* National Institute of Justice. www.ncjrs.gov/pdffiles1/Digitization/111964NCJRS.pdf

Eysink Smeets, M., Van't Hof, K., Beijers, G., Van der Kemp, J., Van Os, P. & Versteegh, P. (2010) *Probleemgericht werken en de rol van criminaliteitsanalyse in 60 kleine stappen.* www.inholland.nl/onderzoek/publicaties/probleemgericht-werken-en-de-rol-van-criminaliteitsanalyse-in-60-kleine-stappen. Translation by: Clarke, R.V., & Eck, J.E. (2010). Crime Analysis for Problem Solvers In 60 Small Steps.

Farrell, G. (2013). Five tests for a theory of the crime drop. *Crime Science, 2(1), p. 5.*

Farrell, G, Tilley, N. & Tseloni, A. (2014) 'Why the Crime Drop?' *Crime and Justice 43: 421-490.*

Farrell, G., Tseloni, A. & Chenevoy, N. (2018). 'Did violence fall after property crime?' *G. Farrell and A. Sidebottom (Eds). (2018). Realistic Evaluation for Crime Science: Essays in Honour of Nick Tilley. London: Taylor and Francis. (p. 141-155).*

Farrell, G., Tseloni, A. & Tilley, N. (2011). The Effectiveness of VeHICle Security Devices and their Role in the Crime Drop. *Criminology and Criminal Justice 11(1): 21-35.*

Farrington, D. & Welsh, B. (2002). Effects of improved street lighting on crime: a systematic review. *Home Office Research Study 251.*

Ferwerda, H. & Van Wijk, A. (2010). De actieradius van problematische jeugdgroepen. *F. Bovenkerk, M. Easton, L. Gunther Moor & P. Ponsaers (eds.), Policing multiple communities. Cahiers Politie-studies, 2 (p. 159-168).* Maklu.

Ferwerda, H., Beke, B. & Bervoets, E. (2013). *Jeugdgroepen van toen. Een casusonderzoek naar de leden van drie criminele jeugdgroepen uit het einde van de vorige eeuw.* Politie & Wetenschap.

Ferwerda, H & Van Ham, T. (2015) *Problematische Jeugdgroepen in Nederland. Omvang en aard in het najaar van 2014.* Bureau Beke, Arnhem https://www.bureaubeke.nl/doc/2015/Prob_jeugdgoep_najaar_2014.pdf

Ferwerda, H., Beke, B. & Bervoets, E. (2017). De onzichtbare invloed van bovenlokale criminele netwerken op de wijk. *Tijdschrift voor de Politie – jg.79, nr.9/10, 11.*

Fijnaut, C. & Rovers, B. (2016). *De aanpak van overvallen en overvallers in de jaren 2011-2016: Een gegronde beschouwing over de resultaten en vooruitzichten.*

FRA. (2014). *European Union Agency for Fundamental Rights (FRA) on Violence against women.* https://fra.europa.eu/en/publication/2014/violence-against-women-eu-wide-survey-main-results-report

FRA. (2021). *European Union Agency for Fundamental Rights (2021) CRIME, SAFETY, AND VICTIMS' RIGHTS.* Luxembourg: Publications Office of the European Union, 2021 See for comparable victim surveys also the predecessor of FRA-2021: the International Crime Victim Survey (ICVS; https://wp.unil.ch/icvs/)

Municipality of Rotterdam. (z.d.). *Buurt Bestuurt.* www.rotterdam.nl/wonen-leven/buurt-bestuurt/

Gonzalez Fuster, G. (2020). *Artificial Intelligence and Law Enforcement: Impact on Fundamental Rights.* Brussels: European Parliament. www.europarl.europa.eu/RegData/etudes/STUD/2020/656295/IPOL_STU(2020)656295_EN.pdf

Gstrein, O.J. & Zwitter, A. (2020). Een transparant debat over algoritmen. *Bestuurskunde 2020 (29).*

Grapperhaus, F.B.J. (2019) *Speech by Minister of Justice and Security Grapperhaus at the Congress '10 jaar bestrijding van high impact crimes'*, Rotterdam, De Doelen, 13 mei 2019. www.rijksoverheid.nl/documenten/toespraken/2019/05/13/toespraak-minister-grapperhaus-congres-%E2%80%9910-jaar-bestrijding-van-high-impact-crimes%E2%80%99

Guerette, R.T. (2009). Analyzing Crime Displacement and Diffusion. *Tool Guide No. 10.* https://popcenter.asu.edu/content/analyzing-crime-displacement-and-diffusion

Hesseling, R.B.P. (1994). *Stoppen of verplaatsen?* WODC 137. Gouda Quint. Home Office (2020) Safer Streets Fund – Crime Prevention toolkit January 2020 https://assets.publishing.service.gov.uk/government/uploads/system/uploads/attachment_data/file/860797/safer-streets-fund-prospectus.pdf

The CCV. (2009). *Hoe doen ze het toch? Modus Operandi Woninginbraak.* https://hetccv.nl/onderwerpen/woninginbraak/documenten/hoe-doen-ze-het-toch-modus-operandi-woninginbraak/

ICVS: International Crime Victim Survey. (z.d.). *Publications.* https://wp.unil.ch/icvs/key-publications/

ISO. (2018). *ISO 31000:2018 (en) Risk management – Guidelines.* www.iso.org/standard/65694.html

ISO. (2021). *ISO 22341:2021 (en) Security and resilience — Protective security — Guidelines for crime prevention through environmental design.* www.iso.org/standard/50078.html

Jeurissen, E. & Vriesde, R. (2012). Co-creatie 2.0. Strategische kansen voor de innovatieve politiepraktijk. *Chapter 4, from page 79.* www.politieacademie.nl/kennisenonderzoek/kennis/mediatheek/PDF/86862.PDF

Jongejan, A. (2020). *Presentatie CCI (2020): The Dutch 'Police Label Secure Housing': A Successful Approach.*

Jongejan, A. & Woldendorp, T. (2013). A Successful CPTED Approach: The Dutch 'Police Label Secure Housing' Built Environment. *Vol. 39, No. 1, Planning for Crime Prevention: An International Perspective (2013), p. 31-48.* Alexandrine Press. www.jstor.org/stable/43296831

Kleemans, E. R. & Van Koppen, M. V. (2014). Careers in organized crime. *Encyclopedia of Criminology and Criminal Justice 285–295.* Geciteerd (p. 7) in Weisburd, D., Savona, E.U., Hasisi, B., Calderoni, F. editors (2020). Understanding Recruitment to Organized Crime and Terrorism. Springer.

Kolb, D. A. (1984). *Experiential Learning: experience as the source of learning and development.* Englewood Cliffs: Prentice Hall.

Kolb. D. A., & Fry, R. (1975). Towards an applied theory of experiential learning. *In C. Cooper (Ed.), Theories of Group Process.* John Wiley.

Korthals Altes, H.J., Stienstra, H., IJmker, A., Van Soomeren, P. & Van der Gugten, M. (1993). *Naar een Politiekeurmerk Veilig Wonen; voorstudie 'Secured by Design' in Nederland.* DSP-groep.

Kuitert, K. & Woldendorp, T. (2009). *Advies sociale veiligheid parkeergarage Karperton, Alkmaar.* DSP-groep.

Kunst, M.J.J., Van Dijk, J.J.M., Pemberton, A. & Bruinsma, M.Y.(2008). *Preventie van herhaald slachtofferschap; een research synthese van maatregelen ter voorkoming van herhaling.* WODC, UvT, Intervict, Tilburg.

Lam, J.M., Rottenberg, A., Sinke, M.A.R., Tigchelaar, E.Y. & Kop, N. (2017). *Integraal werken loont, onderzoek naar de veiligheidsstrategie B3W bij woninginbraken.* Boom Criminologie.

Lopez, M. (2007). *Besmettelijke woninginbraken.* Politie en Wetenschap. In collaboration with: the Hollands Midden & Noord-Holland-Noord police forces. www.politieenwetenschap.nl/cache/files/5f7dfa7946835besmettelijke_woninginbraken.pdf

Lopez, M. (red.), De Bonth, I., Verhagen, D., Van Nes, A. & Waaijer, S. (2013). *Sociaal Veilige Stedenbouw; de ruimtelijke potenties van de Alkmaarse buurten Vroonermeer-Noord en -Zuid.* www.researchgate.net/publication/323676857_Sociaal_Veilige_Stedenbouw_De_ruimtelijke_potenties_van_de_Alkmaarse_buurten_Vroonermeer-Noord_en_-Zuid

Luten, I. (red.), (2008). Sociale Veiligheid in buitenruimten, gebouwen en woningen. *Handboek Veilig Ontwerp en Beheer – p. 31.* Uitgeverij Toth.

Mali, B., Bronkhorst-Giesen, C. & Den Hengst, M. (2017). *Predictive policing: lessen voor de toekomst'. Een evaluatie van de landelijke pilot.* Politie Academie.

Martens, P. (2015). *Veiligheid in parkeergarages.*
www.vexpan.nl/wp-content/uploads/2015/11/Vexpansie3-veiligh.-in-P-garages.pdf

Netherlands Ministry of Justice and Security. (2019). Uitwerking Veiligheidsagenda 2019 - 2022. Vastgesteld in het LOVP van 3 december 2018. *Publication no. 118843, Chapter 3b.*

Movisie. (2019). *Evidence-based werken is geen keurslijf.*
www.movisie.nl/artikel/evidence-based-werken-geen-keurslijf

Nauta, O (2004). *De effectiviteit van het Politiekeurmerk Veilig Wonen®.* DSP-groep, Amsterdam.

Netherlands Public Prosecution Service (2020). *Richtlijnenbundel, version 0.12.*

Oriënteringsnota Voorkoming Misdrijven (1981). Bureau Landelijk Coördinator Voorkoming Misdrijven, 's-Gravenhage (Netherlands Ministries of Justice and Security and of the Interior and Kingdom Relations).

Pawson, R. & Tilley, N. (2004). *Realistic Evaluation.* Sage Publications, London, Thousand Oaks en New Delhi.

Perry, W.L., McInnis, B., Price, C.C., Smith, S.C., & Hollywood, J.S. (2013). *Predictive Policing, The Role of Crime Forecasting in Law Enforcement Operations.* Rand Safety and Justice Program. Predictive Policing: The Role of Crime Forecasting in Law Enforcement Operations (rand.org)

Peeck, V., Van Mantgem, J. & Ter Woerds, S. (2018). Kwetsbare vluchtelingen; Slachtofferschap onder de radar. *Tijdschrift voor de Politie – jg.80/nr.6/18.*
www.politieacademie.nl/kennisenonderzoek/kennis/mediatheek/pdf/94815.pdf

Politieacademie. (2013). *Informatiegestuurd politiewerk.*
www.politieacademie.nl/thema/gebiedsgebondenpolitie/canonggp/
planmatigenmethodischwerken/Paginas/Informatiegestuurd-politiewerk.aspx

Politieacademie. (2013). *Integraal veiligheidsbeleid.*
www.politieacademie.nl/thema/gebiedsgebondenpolitie/canonggp/
gemeenschappelijkeveiligheidsaanpak/Paginas/Integraal-veiligheidsbeleid.aspx

Politieacademie. (2014). https://thesaurus.politieacademie.nl/Thesaurus/Term/5117.

Querbach, M., Krom, M., & Jongejan, A. (2019). *Review of State of the Art: Predictive Policing. Onderdeel van het Europese H2020 project – Cutting Crime Impact (CCI).*

Ratcliffe, J.H. (2016) *Intelligence-Led Policing.* **Routledge.**

Rau. M. & Neri, A. (2019). *La Nube de los Sueños; un ejercicio de diagnóstico infantil Zacatecas Government in Mexico.* https://pbk.cl/pbk-webSite/wp-content/
uploads/2021/04/Manual-Instructivo-Taller-de-los-Sueños.pdf

Rau, M. (2021). Digital Child Perception Diagnosis the 'Cloud of Dreams'. *The ICA Newsletter April-June 2021. The International CPTED Association, Volume 17 Issue 2.* https://www.
cpted.net/resources/Documents/ICA%20Resources/Newsletters/The%20ICA%20
Newsletter-June%202021.pdf

Regionaal Samenwerkingsverband Integrale Veiligheid.(2017). *Naar een duurzame afname van woninginbraken. Vastgesteld in het Regionaal Bestuurlijk Overleg van de Eenheid Den Haag op 29 juni 2017.* https://rsiv.nl/action/?action=download&id=124

Rijksoverheid. (Government of The Netherlands). (2019). *Speech by minister Grapperhaus at the Congress '10 jaar bestrijding van high impact crimes'* https://www.rijksoverheid.nl/
documenten/toespraken/2019/05/13/toespraak-minister-grapperhaus-congres-'10-jaar-
bestrijding-van-high-impact-crimes'

Rovers, B., Bruinsma, M., Jacobs, M., Jans, M., Moors, H., Siesling, M., & Fijnaut, C. (2010). *Overvallen in Nederland; een fenomeenanalyse en evaluatie van de aanpak.* **Boom Juridische Uitgevers.**

Schrijer, D. (2019). *Groeien aan de Maas. De verbindende kracht van Vitale Coalities.* www.vtw.nl/data/media/files/Essay_Dominic_Schrijver_over_de_kracht_van_
verbinding_in_vitale_coalities.pdf **Also see: Vos, L. (no date). Toezichthouders moeten rugdekking geven - interview met Dominic Schrijer over vitale coalities.** *Vereniging van toezichthouders in woningcorporaties (VTW), Newsletter 155, Article 1210.* www.vtw.nl/
nieuwsbrief/155/artikel/1210

Shaw, I.F., Greene, J.C. & Mark, M.M. (2006). *The SAGE Handbook of Evaluation.* Sage Publications, London, Thousand Oaks and New Delhi.

Sherman, L.W. (2020). *How to Count Crime: the Cambridge Harm Index Consensus.* https://doi.org/10.1007/s41887-020-00043-2

Sherman, L.W., Gottfredson, D., Mackenzie, D., Eck, J., Reuter, P. & Bushways, S. (1997). *Preventing crime: What Works, What Doesn't, What's Promising.* https://www.semanticscholar.org/paper/Preventing-Crime%3A-What-Works%2C-What-Doesn't%2C-What's-Sherman-Gottfredson/5e82dc4c3c8a913687747b41f452806a48b0db76#related-papers)

Sidebottom, A., Bullock, K., Armitage, R., Ashby, M., Clemmow, C., Kirby, S., Laycock, G. & Tilley, N. (2019). *Problem-Oriented Policing in England and Wales 2019.* Ryton-on-Dunsmore: College of Policing. https://www.researchgate.net/publication/340540699_Problem-Oriented_Policing_in_England_and_Wales_2019

Stol, W., Tielenburg, C., Rodenhuis, W., Kolthoff, E., Van Duin, M. & Veenstra, S. (2016). *Basisboek integrale veiligheid.* Boom.

Taskforce Overvallen. (2011). *Actieprogramma ketenaanpak overvalcriminaliteit.*

Terpstra, J. & Van Dijk, B. (2014). *Probleemgerichte aanpak van woninginbraken Beresteinlaan; nuttige lessen na één jaar.* The Hague police unit/DSP-groep Amsterdam.

Van Baardewijk, J., Van den Brink, G. J. M., & Van Os, P. (Eds.) (2007). *Meer heterdaadkracht: 'Aanhoudend in de buurt.* Politieacademie.

Van den Handel, C., Nauta, O., Van Soomeren, P. Van Amersfoort, P, (2009) *Hoe doen ze het toch?*

Modus Operandi Woninginbraak Eindrapportage. CCV/DSP-groep, Utrecht/Amsterdam.

Van den Oord, S. & Kokkeler, B. (2020). Digitale coproductie van preventie en opsporing met burgers. Een verkenning naar de contouren van een nieuw beleidsregime. *Tijdschrift voor Veiligheid 2020 (19).*

Van der Zwet, R. (2018). *Implementing evidence-based practice in social work: a shared responsibility.* www.movisie.nl/sites/movisie.nl/files/2018-11/Implementing-evidence-based-practice-in-social-work.pdf

Van Dijk, J.J.M., Tseloni, A. & Farrell, G. (2012). *The International Crime Drop, New Directions in Research.*

Van Dijk, J.J.M., Van Soomeren, P. & De Waard, J. (2017). Safeguarding Sustainable Crime Prevention: The Rocky Case of the Netherlands. *Crime Prevention: International Perspectives, Issues, and Trends Editors: John A. Winterdyk.* DOI: 10.1201/9781315314211-19

Van Dijk, B., Terpstra, J. & Hulshof, P. (2013). Samenvatting Heterdaadkracht in twee Haagse pilotgebieden. *Politiekunde 55, Politie en Wetenschap.* www.politieenwetenschap.nl/ publicatie/politiekunde/2013/heterdaadkracht-in-twee-haagse-pilotgebieden-13/

Van Dijk, B., Van den Handel, C. & Versteegh, P. (2011). *Hot spotaanpak in vier stappen.* https://www.dsp-groep.nl/wp-content/uploads/11bdstapin_Hot_spotaanpak_vier_ stappen_politie-Haaglanden-_DSP-groep.pdf

Van Dijk, J.J.M., Sagel-Grande, H.I. & Toornvliet, L.G. (2006). Actuele Criminologie. *Hoofdstuk 6 Criminaliteitspreventie, 5th revised edition..* SDU.

Van Dijk, J.M. & De Waard, J. (1991). A Two-Dimensional Typology of Crime Prevention Projects; With a Bibliography. *Typology of Crime Prevention Projects (p. 483-503).*

Van Dijk, T. & Versteegh, P. (2015). *Handleiding B3W-vragenlijst.* https://rsiv.nl/ action/?action=download&id=126

Van Dijk, T., Van Musscher, P. & Versteegh, P. (2015). Doen wat nodig is, kwalitatieve sturing en verantwoording. *Cahiers Politiestudies (ISSN: 1784-5300), 37.* www.maklu-online.eu/nl/ tijdschrift/cahiers-politiestudies/jaargang-2015/37-verantwoording-en-politie/doen-wat- nodig-kwalitatieve-sturing-en-verantwoord/

Van Egmond, P., Swami-Persaud, A. & Verwest, A. (2020). *Q-teams; De politie onderweg naar toekomstbestendige opsporing en vervolging.* Politie en Wetenschap: Sdu Uitgevers.

Van Grinsven, S., & Verwest, A. (2017). Vijf jaar Aanpak Top600: waar staan we nu? *Justitiële verkenningen, jrg. 43, nr. 1, 127-141.*

Van Kalshoven, F. (2021). Als er geen doel is kun je ook niet scoren (of missen). *Volkskrant, 15 May 2021, p. 17.*

Van Ours, J.C. & Vollaard, B. (2011) Does Regulation of Built-in Security Reduce Crime? Evidence from a Natural Experiment. *The Economic Journal, Volume 121, Issue 552. May 2011, p. 485-504.*

Van Reemst, L. Fisher, T.F.C. & Van Dongen, J.D.M. (2013). *Risicofactoren voor herhaald slachtofferschap: Een literatuurscan.* Sectie Criminologie, Erasmus School of Law.

Van Soomeren, P. & Wever, J. (2015). *Review of costs and benefits analysis in crime prevention Report to the European Commission.* Directorate-General for Justice, Freedom and Security; Contract JAI/B/1/2003/05a. Accessed via www.researchgate.net/publication/341110676_Review_of_Costs_and_Benefits_Analysis_in_Crime_Prevention_Report_to_ the_European_Commission_Directorate-General_for_Justice_Freedom_and_Security_Contract_ JAIB1200305a

Van der Velpen, P. (2018). *Het preventie ultimatum.* Uitgeverij SWP.

Van der Vijver, K., Johannink, R., Overal, K., Slot, P., Vermeer, A., Van der Werff, P., Willekens, H. & Wisman, F. (2009). *Burgernet in de praktijk. De evaluatie van de pilot Burgernet.* Stichting Maatschappij Veiligheid en Politie (SMVP), Dordrecht. https://maatschappijenveiligheid.nl/kennisbank/burgernet/

Veilig@Rotterdam. (2018). *High Impact Crime 2019 Rotterdam.* Municipality of Rotterdam.

Veilig@Rotterdam. (2018). *Veiligheidsprogramma 2018 – 2023.* Municipality of Rotterdam.

Veilig010. (2013). *Programma veiligheid 2014-2018.* Municipality of Rotterdam.

Vereniging van Nederlandse Gemeenten (2021). *Kernbeleid Veiligheid; Handreiking voor gemeenten.*

Vereniging van Nederlandse Gemeenten & Ministerie van Buitenlandse Zaken en Koninkrijksrelaties. (2010). Naar buiten - Spoorboekje burgerparticipatie voor raad en college. *Uitgave van In actie met burgers!, deelproject van het Actieprogramma Lokaal Bestuur.* https://vng.nl/files/vng/vng/Documenten/Extranet/Burgerzaken/bestanden_burgerparticipatie/Naar_buiten.pdf

Versteegh, P. (2005). *Informatie Gestuurde Veiligheidszorg.* Stichting SMVP.

Versteegh, P. & Hesseling, R. (2013). De B3W-matrix, naar een meer effectieve aanpak van woninginbraken. *Tijdschrift voor de Politie, jrg. 75, nr. 9/10, 15-21.* Reed Business Information. www.politieacademie.nl/kennisenonderzoek/kennis/mediatheek/pdf/89054.pdf

Verwest, A. (2016). *Aanpak Top600 en het Actiecentrum Veiligheid.* www.dsp-groep.nl/projecten/aanpak-top600-actiecentrum-veiligheid/

VNG. (2021). *Handreiking voor gemeenten - Kernbeleid Veiligheid 2021.*

Wegwijzer jeugd en veiligheid. (z.d.). *Jeugdgroepen aanpakken: gebruik het 7 stappenmodel.*

Weisburd, D., Savona, E.U., Hasisi, B. & Calderoni, F. editors (2020). *Understanding Recruitment to Organized Crime and Terrorism.* Springer.

Welten, B.J.A.M. (2005). *Politie in ontwikkeling: visie op de politiefunctie.* Stichting SMVP.

Wolfgang, M. & Sellin, T. (1964). *The measurement of delinquency.* Wiley and Sons. https://journals.sagepub.com/doi/abs/10.1177/001112876501100417?journalCode=cadc

Wolfowicz, M., Litmanovitz, Y., Weisburd, D. & Hasisi, B. (2019). A Field-Wide Systematic Review and Meta-analysis of Putative Risk and Protective Factors for Radicalization Outcomes. *Journal of Quantitative Criminology, 3 December, 1-41.* https://link.springer.com/article/10.1007/s10940-019-09439-4

WRR. (2016). *Big Data in een vrije en veilige samenleving. Report no. 95.* www.wrr.nl/publicaties/rapporten/2016/04/28/big-data-in-een-vrije-en-veilige-samenleving

WRR. (2016). *Factsheet aanbevelingen WRR-rapport 95: Big Data in een vrije en veilige samenleving.* www.wrr.nl/publicaties/rapporten/2016/04/28/big-data-in-een-vrije-en-veilige-samenleving

WRR. (2016). *Synopsis van WRR-rapport 95: Big Data in een vrije en veilige samenleving.* www.wrr.nl/publicaties/rapporten/2016/04/28/big-data-in-een-vrije-en-veilige-samenleving

Websites ↗

www.cuttingcrimeimpact.eu

www.ProHIC.nl

https://data.politie.nl/#/Politie/nl

https://beveiligingnieuws.nl/achtergrond/terugblik-op-tien-jaar-succesvolle-aanpak-high-impact-crime

Secondant: Het wordt veiliger in Nederland, maar niet overal (www.ccv-secondant.nl)

www.youtube.com/watch?v=2Groq98rQyA&list=PLZ0df6wQ5oO85B_LIIJSSu7pQfruMOvjf&index=5&t=0s

www.youtube.com/watch?v=QVVRF_cwJr0&list=PLZ0df6wQ5oO85B_LIIJSSu7pQfruMOvjf&index=5

www.burgemeesters.nl/bevoegdheden/politiewet

https://nl.wikipedia.org/wiki/Driehoek_(overheid)

www.zorgenveiligheidshuizen.nl

https://hetccv.nl/onderwerpen/high-impact-crimes/HIC-preventiewijzer/

www.zorgenveiligheidshuizen.nl/nieuws/2020/240320_animatie-zorg-en-veiligheidshuizen

www.riec.nl